Houghton
Mifflin
Harcourt

PERFORMANCE ASSESSMENT

6

Approaching Performance Assessments with Confidence

By Carol Jago

In order to get good at anything, you need to practice. Whether the goal is to improve your jump shot, level up in a video game, or make the cut in band tryouts, success requires repeated practice on the court, computer, and field. The same is true of reading and writing. The only way to get good at them is by reading and writing.

Malcolm Gladwell estimates in his book *Outliers* that mastering a skill requires about 10,000 hours of dedicated practice. He argues that individuals who are outstanding in their field have one thing in common—many, many hours of working at it. Gladwell claims that success is less dependent on innate talent than it is on practice. Now I'm pretty sure that I could put in 10,000 hours at a ballet studio and still be a terrible dancer, but I agree with Gladwell that, "Practice isn't the thing you do once you're good. It's the thing you do that makes you good."

Not just any kind of practice will help you master a skill, though. Effective practice needs to focus on improvement. That is why this series of reading and writing tasks begins with a model of the kind of reading and writing you are working towards, then takes you through practice exercises, and finally invites you to perform the skills you have practiced.

Once through the cycle is only the beginning. You will want to repeat the process many times over until close reading, supporting claims with evidence, and crafting a compelling essay is something you approach with confidence. Notice that I didn't say "with ease." I wish it were otherwise, but in my experience as a teacher and as an author, writing well is never easy.

The work is worth the effort. Like a star walking out on the stage, you put your trust in the hours you've invested in practice to result in thundering applause. To our work together!

Unit 1 Argumentative Essay
Animal and Human Interactions

STEP 1 ANALYZE THE MODEL

Should animals be kept in zoos?

Read Source Materials

STEP 2 PRACTICE THE TASK

*Should people be allowed to keep
pit bulls as pets?*

Read Source Materials

Write an Argumentative Essay

STEP 3 PERFORM THE TASK

Can animals learn or use language?

Read Source Materials

Unit 2 Informative Essay
Disaster!

STEP 1 ANALYZE THE MODEL

*What causes home fires and how can
we prevent them?*

Read Source Materials

© Houghton Mifflin Harcourt Publishing Company • Image Credits: ©Jupiterimages/Getty Images; ©Todd Klassy/Sutterstock

© Houghton Mifflin Harcourt Publishing Company • Image Credits: ©Mick Roessler/Corbis; ©Jupiterimages/Getty Images

Unit 3 Literary Analysis
Viewpoints

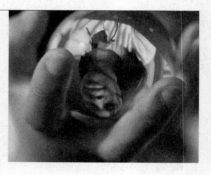

Unit 4 Mixed Practice
On Your Own

© Houghton Mifflin Harcourt Publishing Company • Image Credits:

Animal and Human Interactions

Argumentative Essay

ANALYZE THE MODEL

Evaluate an essay about keeping animals in zoos.

PRACTICE THE TASK

Write an essay about whether or not people should have pet pit bulls.

PERFORM THE TASK

Write an essay about animals' ability to learn or use language.

Think about the last time you tried to convince someone about something. To make your point, you used reasons or examples to support your position. Although a formal argument is different from a conversational argument, they share some basic qualities.

The ability to sway, convince, or change someone's opinion is a powerful communication tool. By presenting your argument in a way that is persuasive, you are expressing your point of view using facts, logic, and reason.

IN THIS UNIT, you will learn how to write an argumentative essay that is based on your close reading and analysis of several relevant sources. You will learn a step-by-step approach to stating a claim—and then organizing your essay to support your claim in a clear and logical way.

ANALYZE THE MODEL

Should animals be kept in zoos?

You will read:

▶ **TWO INFORMATIONAL ARTICLES**

Zoos and Aquariums Have a Positive Impact on Visitors

Do Zoos Shorten Elephant Life Spans?

You will analyze:

▶ **A STUDENT MODEL**
Have You Ever Seen an Elephant?

Source Materials for Step 1

The following texts were used by Mrs. Renee's student, Justin Rivers, as sources for his essay, "Have You Ever Seen an Elephant?" As you read, make notes in the side columns and underline information that you find useful.

NOTES

Zoos and Aquariums Have a Positive Impact on Visitors

BY OLIVER DUNHILL, *zoo and aquarium manager*

Organizations such as the Association of Zoos and Aquariums (AZA) recently conducted a study to find out if zoos and aquariums make a lasting impact on visitors. The study showed that people are positively affected by their experiences at zoos and aquariums. Knowing what visitors take away from the experience can show that visiting these establishments encourages people to be more aware of their attitudes toward conservation. Visitors also improve their understanding of exotic animals and the environments these animals live in.

Zoos and aquariums that are recognized by the AZA, including the two I manage, work to actively educate their visitors. We offer lectures and show videos that feature some of the animals in the zoo and the aquarium. The topics can cover an animal's natural environment, what its diet is, or what dangers it faces from human presence.

These programs might be the only time that adult visitors learn about why plastic bags are dangerous to sea turtles and birds, for example. The information they learn in these programs could inspire them to research more about the animal or the dangers its species faces in the wild.

People who visit zoos think more positively about conservation. Many visitors will feel a stronger connection to nature after their visit and are more likely to reflect on their role in protecting the environment.

1. Analyze   2. Practice   3. Perform

Do Zoos Shorten Elephant Life Spans?

by Virginia Morell

Elephants are one of the top draws for zoos, which are the only places most of us get a chance to see the behemoths.[1] But a new and controversial study in *Science* suggests that captivity is so bad for female elephants' health and overall well-being that their life spans are less than that of half of those of protected populations in Africa and Asia. The data also indicate that captive-born Asian elephant calves are particularly likely to die young. The team has called for an end to zoos' acquisition of wild elephants and for limits on transfers of animals among zoos.

Already concerned about their elephants, many zoos in the United States and Europe are expanding or building new enclosures, or even deciding against exhibiting the great beasts altogether. Studies in the wild have documented the importance of roaming and family ties for these animals, which zoos with limited space often cannot provide.

Some of the zoo elephants' problems stem from the practices of removing young calves from their mothers and transferring females from one zoo to another, usually for breeding. Both practices break the animals' family ties and presumably cause mental stress. "In the wild, females always stay with their mothers; they never leave the herd where they're born," says Mason. Zoo elephants are often overweight as well, due to a lack of space in which to roam.

---

[1] **behemoth** an enormous creature or animal

Discuss and Decide

You have read two sources about the relationships between people, animals, and zoos. Without going any further, discuss the question: Should animals be kept in zoos?

Analyze a Student Model for Step 1

Read Justin's argumentative essay closely. The red side notes are the comments that his teacher, Mrs. Renee, wrote.

Justin Rivers
Mrs. Renee
English 6
October 15

Have You Ever Seen an Elephant?

Good intro! The two questions draw your readers in.

Have you ever heard the roar of a lion? Have you ever seen elephants so close that you could practically touch them? If you have, most likely you saw these great creatures in a zoo.

This works well to set up your argument.

Watch out! If some people get their way, most zoos everywhere will be abolished. Try to imagine a world where lions and tigers and elephants can be seen only in old films and photo books.

Good transition to the threat of closing zoos.

Come to think of it, maybe it's better not to imagine such a thing. A world without zoos is scary. Zoos have been around for at least 3500 years. Today more than 600 million people visit the zoos of the world each year. What if all zoos closed down?

What are your sources?

Animal Research and Zoos

I like the heads you used. They offer good support for the reader.

If all zoos shut their gates, the excitement and knowledge they bring to all of us would be gone! However, unhappy children would not be the only problem.

Many large zoos have animal research programs. That makes sense because paying scientists to travel great distances to study animals in the wild is very expensive. It can also be very difficult to get close enough to wild animals to conduct this kind of on-site research. In fact, zoos raise a significant amount of the money that is spent on the research to save animals.

1. Analyze   2. Practice   3. Perform

© Houghton Mifflin Harcourt Publishing Company • Image Credits: © Elvele Images Ltd/Alamy

Breeding and Zoos

Very rare animals in the wild are often rare for a reason. Sometimes their environment is being destroyed, or they are losing the competition with the needs of people.

Some large zoos have breeding programs to keep rare animals from going extinct. Some of these zoos even have programs to return animals they have bred to the wild.

Your explanations are clear.

Fairness

Zoos give my friends and me a chance to learn about animals. Without zoos, only very wealthy families would be able to visit animals in the wild! My family can't travel to Africa or the Galapagos Islands, but we *can* go to the zoo.

Closing zoos would not be fair to endangered animals either. Because of zoos, more people know how to help animals that can't help themselves. After all, many animal species need us to care because they can't solve their own problems. What can wild animals do about curing their own diseases, finding water during a drought, or finding food when their territories are shrinking?

Interesting point about fairness! Well done, Justin.

Good image.

Many zoos have education programs that put a spotlight on animals that need help and environments that are at risk. When people know what they can do to help out, they often do it.

Well written.

Facing the Argument

Those who are against zoos point out that of the 10,000 zoos around the world, many keep the animals in bad conditions. Some zoos do not provide the animals with the things they need to live naturally, such as plenty of space to roam and the chance to hunt. However, the main objections to zoos could be solved by forcing government agencies to check regularly on animals in zoos. Animals deserve this help. And we deserve the chance to see them up close.

Consider using a noun.

Discuss and Decide

Did Justin convince you that zoos are worthwhile? If so, cite the compelling evidence in his essay.

Terminology of Argumentative Texts

Read each term and explanation. Then look back at Justin Rivers' argumentative essay and find an example to complete the chart.

Term	Explanation	Example from Justin's Essay
audience	The **audience** for your argument is a group of people that you want to convince. As you develop your argument, consider your audience's knowledge level and concerns.	
purpose	The **purpose** for writing an argument is to sway the audience. Your purpose should be clear, whether it is to persuade your audience to agree with your claim, or to motivate your audience to take some action.	
precise claim	A **precise claim** confidently states your viewpoint. Remember that you must be able to find reasons and evidence to support your claim, and that you must distinguish your claim from opposing claims.	
reason	A **reason** is a statement that supports your claim. (You should have more than one reason.) Note that you will need to supply evidence for each reason you state.	
opposing claim	An **opposing claim,** or **counterclaim,** shares the point of view of people who do not agree with your claim. Opposing claims must be fairly presented with evidence.	

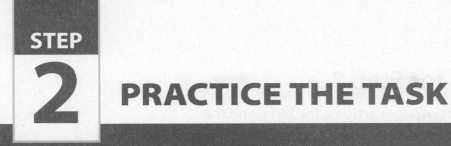

Should people be allowed to keep pit bulls as pets?

You will read:

▶ **TWO NEWSPAPER ARTICLES**
Ohio Overturns Pit Bull Bill

Miami-Dade County Votes to Keep Pit Bulls Out

▶ **A BLOG**
Pit Bulls Haven't Always Had a Bad Rep

▶ **A NEWSPAPER EDITORIAL**
The Media and the Pit Bull

You will write:

▶ **AN ARGUMENTATIVE ESSAY**
Should people be allowed to keep pit bulls as pets?

Source Materials for Step 2

AS YOU READ Analyze the newspaper articles, the blog, and the editorial. Annotate the sources with notes that help you decide where you stand on the issue: Should people be allowed to keep pit bulls as pets?

Source 1: Newspaper Article

OHIO OVERTURNS PIT BULL BILL

February 21, 2012

COLUMBUS—The Ohio State Legislature voted today on a bill to eliminate a 25-year-old law automatically declaring pit bulls as vicious. The original bill, enacted in 1987, was the only state law in the country to discriminate against a specific breed—the pit bull.

Under the old law, owners of all pit bulls were required to register their dogs as *dangerous*. Other dogs were labeled as *vicious* if they had ever injured a person seriously, or killed another dog. However, all pit bulls were automatically included in either the *dangerous* or *vicious* category.

The new bill, House Bill 14, redefines the designations of *vicious* and *dangerous* and creates a lesser category of a *nuisance* dog. In addition to removing any mention of a specific breed, this bill creates a process for dog owners to change labels applied by law enforcement. Now, the legal responsibility for proving that a dog deserves its label is on the dog warden, and this proof must be clear and convincing.

Representative Bruce Goodwin voted against the bill, in part because, as he states, "I am not convinced that a 'pit bull' is a safe animal to have around. The 'pit bull' has the distinction or characteristic that, when they grab on, they don't let go," Mr. Goodwin said. "You can say all you want about all these other breeds, but 'pit bulls' are the choice for drug dealers and other bad folks for a reason."

Close Read

What evidence does Bruce Goodwin cite to support his view that pit bulls are unsafe?

_____

_____

Source 2: Newspaper Article

MIAMI-DADE COUNTY VOTES TO KEEP PIT BULLS OUT

by Roberto Gómez   **September 1, 2012**

Miami-Dade County is the only county in Florida that has any breed-specific law. In 1989, the county instituted a ban on pit bulls. Last month, they voted to keep the ban in place.

The ban was enacted after a pit bull attacked a young girl. A neighbor's pit bull had escaped from the house, and was sitting in the Moreira's driveway when 8-year-old Melissa and her mother returned to the house. The dog viciously attacked Melissa, requiring her to have multiple major reconstructive surgeries in the years following the incident.

The Morerias worked to pass a law that would prevent anyone else from being injured by pit bulls.

At the time, the county supported the ban. However, as the years have gone by, many are reconsidering their stance. One famous advocate for pit bulls, Mark Buehrle of the Marlins, relocated to Broward County in order to keep his family's pit bull.

The protestations of people such as Buehrle have caused county commissioners to rethink the ban, and consider the fairness and necessity of such a law. However, not enough support was mustered to overturn it.

Discuss and Decide

Review the passages in the article that mention opposition to the ban. What does the article suggest some Miami-Dade County pit bull owners will need to do because of the ban? Cite text evidence in your discussion.

Source 3: Blog

pitbull_lover

Famous Pit Bull Owners

Many famous Americans were proud pit bull owners, including:

- Theodore Roosevelt
- Thomas Edison
- Helen Keller

August 14, 2010

👍 Like   👎 Dislike

Pit Bulls Haven't Always Had a Bad Rep

The term "pit bull" doesn't describe a single breed, but multiple breeds of working dogs. Bulldogs and terriers were crossbred to produce these working breeds. The American pit bull terrier, American Staffordshire terrier, and Staffordshire bull terrier make up the core of the "breed." The term is used to reference a variety of muscular dogs with short hair. Many of these short-haired, muscular dogs are mixed breeds that look similar to one another, although they have different genetic backgrounds. Dogs commonly mistaken for pit bulls are mastiffs, boxers, and American bulldogs.

Before the Civil War, when the first pit bulls were brought to America by English and Irish immigrants, they were a respected breed. As working dogs, they were kept as hunters and guardians, as well as herders and pets.

In the early 1900s, the pit bull was one of the most popular breeds in America. Pit bulls became a symbol of American pride, and their image was used on posters to recruit soldiers during World War I. One example of the popularity of pit bulls was Stubby, a pit bull mix who captured the nation's heart during the war.

Stubby was the unofficial mascot of the 102nd Infantry Division. He once saved his entire platoon by warning them of a poison gas attack. Wounded twice in combat, he was the first dog to be awarded Army medals! Stubby came home to a hero's welcome. He is the inspiration behind the U.S. Military's K-9 Corps.

Pit bulls remained popular during the 1950s and 60s, as respected companies used pit bulls as their mascots and in advertising. So it wasn't until the latter part of this century that pit bulls began to acquire their bad rep.

Discuss and Decide

Review the reasons the blog gives for the enduring popularity of pit bulls. Which reasons suggest that a pit bull may make a good pet?

THE MEDIA AND THE PIT BULL

by James Cross   **May 28, 2012**

When I walk my two-year-old pit bull mix, people cross the street to avoid us. When I told my friends about my plan to adopt Maisy from a shelter, many of them said, "They're dangerous! That's like bringing a cat to a chicken coop! You are asking for trouble." Some of my relatives even stopped coming to my house; I'm not so sure that is a bad thing. But it does make me wonder: why do so many people hate pit bulls?

I place the blame squarely in the lap of the media. According to the ASPCA (American Society for the Prevention of Cruelty to Animals), news outlets consistently tell animal control officers that they will not cover a dog attack unless the situation involves a pit bull. Despite the fact that other breeds of dogs can and do attack people, these incidents go unmentioned in the news, even at the local level.

The media intentionally over-reports incidents involving pit bulls, while keeping silent on attacks committed by dogs with better reputations, such as Labradors. News outlets also erroneously report dog attacks. If a dog's breed is unknown, news media will often call it a pit bull. Any short-haired, stocky dog could be mistakenly called a pit bull in the news. People expect to hear about attacks by pit bulls, so the distinction is lost on those hearing the news report. Even if it is later revealed that the dog was not in fact a pit bull, the damage is done, and the idea of the pit bull as a dangerous breed is reinforced in the public eye.

The mistrust of the pit bull, built by media bias, is a cultivated reaction. But we should consider the fact that some of our fear derives from what we have been told—and not by facts.

Close Read

1. What evidence does the author use to support the claim that pit bulls are unfairly targeted in the media? Which expert source does he cite to support his claim?

_____

2. What does *over-report* mean? In what way do the media over-report incidents involving pit pulls? Cite evidence from the text.

_____

Respond to Questions on Step 2 Sources

These questions will help you analyze the sources you've read. Use your notes and refer to the sources in order to answer the questions. Your answers to these questions will help you write your essay.

1 Evaluate the sources. Is the evidence from one source more credible than the evidence from another source? When you evaluate the credibility of a source, consider the expertise of the author and/or the organization responsible for the information. Record your reasons in the chart.

Source	Credible?	Reasons
Newspaper Article Ohio Overturns Pit Bull Bill		
Newspaper Article Miami-Dade County Votes to Keep Pit Bulls Out		
Blog Pit Bulls Haven't Always Had a Bad Rep		
Newspaper Editorial The Media and the Pit Bull		

2 **Prose Constructed-Response** If you were in favor of banning pit bull ownership, which sources would you use to support your view? Cite text evidence in your response.

_____

_____

3 **Prose Constructed-Response** Many different breeds of dogs can bite and hurt people. Should other dog breeds be banned? Cite text evidence in your response.

_____

_____

Types of Evidence

Every reason you offer to support the central claim of your argument must be backed up by evidence. It is useful to think ahead about evidence when you are preparing to write an argument. If you can't find the evidence to support your claim, you will need to revise your claim. The evidence you provide must be relevant, or directly related to your claim. It must also be sufficient. Sufficient evidence is both clear and varied.

Use this chart to help you choose different types of evidence to support your reasons.

Types of Evidence	What Does It Look Like?
Anecdotes: personal examples or stories that illustrate a point	**Blog** "He once saved his entire platoon by warning them of a poison gas attack."
Commonly accepted beliefs: ideas that most people share	**Newspaper Editorial** "The mistrust of the pit bull . . ."
Examples: specific instances or illustrations of a general idea	**Newspaper Article** A neighbor's pit escaped from the house
Expert opinion: statement made by an authority on the subject	**Newspaper Editorial** "According to the ASPCA . . . news outlets consistently tell animal control officers . . ."
Facts: statements that can be proven true, such as statistics or other numerical information	**Newspaper Article** "In 1989, the county instituted a ban on pit bulls."

Planning and Prewriting

Before you draft your essay, complete some important planning steps.

Claim ➡ Reasons ➡ Evidence

 You may prefer to do your planning on a computer.

Make a Precise Claim

1. Should people be allowed to keep pit bulls as pets?

yes ☐   no ☐

2. Review the evidence on pages 10–13. Do the sources support your position?

yes ☐   no ☐

3. If you answered *no* to Question 2, you can either change your position or do additional research to find supporting evidence.

4. State your claim. It should be precise. It should contain the issue and your position on the issue.

Issue: A ban on ownership of pit bulls as pets

Your position on the issue:

_____

Your precise claim:

_____

State Reasons

Next, gather support for your claim. Identify several valid reasons that justify your position.

Reason 1	Reason 2	Reason 3

Find Evidence

You have identified reasons that support your claim. Summarize your reasons in the chart below. Then complete the chart by identifying evidence that supports your reasons.

Relevant Evidence: The evidence you plan to use must be *relevant* to your argument. That is, it should directly and factually support your position.

Sufficient Evidence: Additionally, your evidence must be *sufficient* to make your case. That is, you need to provide enough evidence to convince others.

Short Summary of Reasons	Evidence
Reason 1	Relevant? _____ Sufficient? _____
Reason 2	Relevant? _____ Sufficient? _____
Reason 3	Relevant? _____ Sufficient? _____

Finalize Your Plan

Whether you are writing your essay at home or working in a timed situation at school, it is important to have a plan. You will save time and create a more organized, logical essay by planning the structure before you start writing.

Use your responses on pages 16–17, as well as your close reading notes, to complete the graphic organizer.

▶ Think about how you will grab your reader's attention with an interesting fact or anecdote.

▶ Identify the issue and your position.

▶ State your precise claim.
▶ List the likely opposing claim and how you will counter it.

▶ Restate your claim.

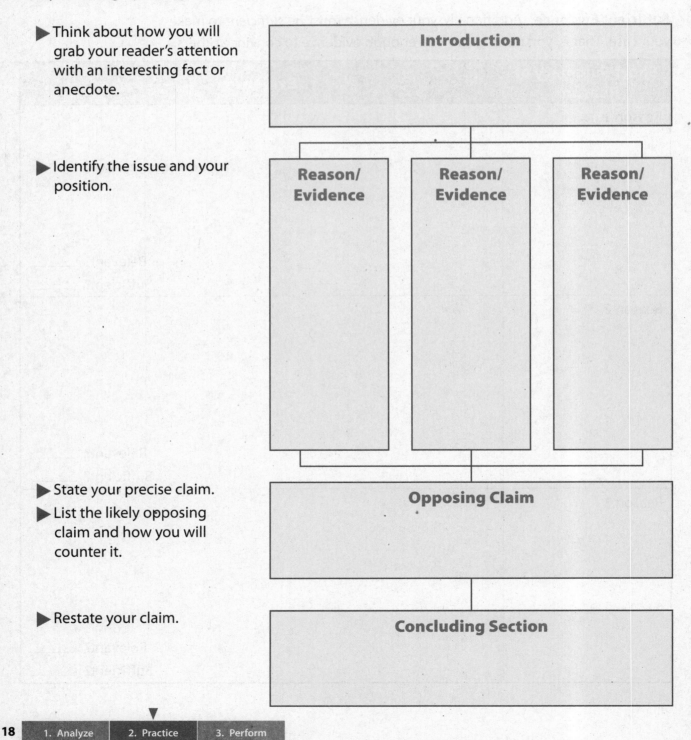

Draft Your Essay

As you write, think about:

▶ **Audience:** Your teacher

▶ **Purpose:** Demonstrate your understanding of the specific requirements of an argumentative essay

▶ **Style:** Use a formal and objective tone that isn't defensive

▶ **Transitions:** Use words, such as *furthermore* or *another reason*, to create cohesion or flow

Revise

Revision Checklist: Self Evaluation

Use the checklist below to guide your analysis.

 If you drafted your essay on the computer, you may wish to print it out so that you can more easily evaluate it.

Ask Yourself	Tips	Revision Strategies
1. Does the introduction grab the audience's attention and include a precise claim?	Draw a wavy line under the attention-grabbing text. Bracket the claim.	Add an attention-grabber. Add a claim or rework the existing one to make it more precise.
2. Do at least two valid reasons support the claim? Is each reason supported by relevant and sufficient evidence?	Underline each reason. Circle each piece of evidence, and draw an arrow to the reason it supports.	Add reasons or revise existing ones to make them more valid. Add relevant evidence to ensure that your support is sufficient.
3. Do transitions create cohesion and link related parts of the argument?	Put a star next to each transition.	Add words, phrases, or clauses to connect related ideas that lack transitions.
4. Are the reasons in the order that is most persuasive?	Number the reasons in the margin, ranking them by their strength and effectiveness.	Rearrange the reasons into a more logical order, such as order of importance.
5. Are opposing claims fairly acknowledged and refuted?	Put a plus sign by any sentence that addresses an opposing claim.	Add sentences that identify and address those opposing claims.
6. Does the concluding section restate the claim?	Put a box around the restatement of your claim.	Add a sentence that restates your claim.

Revision Checklist: Peer Review

Exchange your essay with a classmate, or read it aloud to your partner. As you read and comment on your classmate's essay, focus on logic, organization, and evidence—not on whether you agree with the author's claim. Help each other identify parts of the draft that need strengthening, reworking, or a new approach.

What To Look For	Notes for My Partner
1. Does the introduction grab the audience's attention and include a precise claim?	
2. Do at least two valid reasons support the claim? Is each reason supported by relevant and sufficient evidence?	
3. Do transitions create cohesion and link related parts of the argument?	
4. Are the reasons in the order that is most persuasive?	
5. Are opposing claims fairly acknowledged and refuted?	
6. Does the concluding section restate the claim?	

Edit

Edit your essay to correct spelling, grammar, and punctuation errors.

PERFORM THE TASK

Can animals learn or use language?

You will read:

▶ **TWO MAGAZINE ARTICLES**
Speaking Bonobo

When Animals Communicate, They Are Not Using "Language"

You will analyze:

▶ **A GRAPHIC FEATURE**
What Is Language?

You will write:

▶ **AN ARGUMENTATIVE ESSAY**
Can animals learn or use language?

Part 1: Read Sources

Source 1: Magazine Article

Speaking
BONOBO

by Paul Raffaele

AS YOU READ *Look for evidence that supports your position—or convinces you to change your position on this question: Can animals learn or use language?*

NOTES

SMITHSONIAN MAGAZINE, NOVEMBER 2006

To better understand bonobo intelligence, I traveled to Des Moines, Iowa, to meet Kanzi, a 26-year-old male bonobo reputedly able to converse with humans. When Kanzi was an infant, American psychologist Sue Savage-Rumbaugh tried to teach his mother, Matata, to communicate using a keyboard labeled with geometric symbols. Matata never really got the hang of it, but Kanzi—who usually played in the background, seemingly oblivious, during his mother's teaching sessions— picked up the language.

10 Savage-Rumbaugh and her colleagues kept adding symbols to Kanzi's keyboard and laminated sheets of paper. First Kanzi used 6 symbols, then 18, finally 348. The symbols refer to familiar objects (yogurt, key, tummy, bowl), favored activities (chase, tickle), and even some concepts considered fairly abstract (now, bad).

Kanzi learned to combine these symbols in regular ways, or in what linguists call "proto-grammar." Once, Savage-Rumbaugh says, on an outing in a forest by the Georgia State University laboratory where he was raised, Kanzi touched the 20 symbols for "marshmallow" and "fire." Given matches and marshmallows, Kanzi snapped twigs for a fire, lit them with the matches and toasted the marshmallows on a stick.

1. Analyze 2. Practice 3. Perform

Savage-Rumbaugh claims that in addition to the symbols Kanzi uses, he knows the meaning of up to 3,000 spoken English words. She tests his comprehension in part by having someone in another room pronounce words that Kanzi hears through a set of headphones. Kanzi then points to the appropriate symbol on his keyboard. But Savage-Rumbaugh says Kanzi also understands words that aren't a part of his

30 keyboard vocabulary; she says he can respond appropriately to commands such as "put the soap in the water" or "carry the TV outdoors."

About a year ago, Kanzi and his sister, mother, nephew and four other bonobos moved into a $10 million, 18-room house and laboratory complex at the Great Ape Trust, North America's largest great ape sanctuary, five miles from downtown Des Moines. The bonobo compound boasts a 13,000-square-foot lab, drinking fountains, outdoor playgrounds, rooms linked by hydraulic doors that the animals

40 operate themselves by pushing buttons, and a kitchen where they can use a microwave oven and get snacks from a vending machine (pressing the symbols for desired foods).

Kanzi and the other bonobos spend evenings sprawled on the floor, snacking on M & M's, blueberries, onions and celery, as they watch DVDs they select by pressing buttons on a computer screen. Their favorites star apes and other creatures friendly with humans such as *Quest for Fire, Every Which Way But Loose, Greystoke: The Legend of Tarzan* and *Babe.*

Through a glass panel, Savage-Rumbaugh asks Kanzi if it's

50 OK for me to enter his enclosure. "The bonobos control who comes into their quarters," she explains. Kanzi, still the alpha male of this group in his middle age, has the mien[1] of an aging

© Houghton Mifflin Harcourt Publishing Company

---
[1] **mien** bearing or manner, especially as it reveals an inner state of mind

Close Read

Which details suggest that Kanzi knows 3,000 spoken English words? Cite text evidence in your response.

_____

patriarch—he's balding and paunchy with serious, deep-set eyes. Squealing apparent agreement, he pushes a button, and I walk inside. A wire barrier still separates us. "Kanzi can cause you serious damage if he wants," Savage-Rumbaugh adds.

Kanzi shows me his electronic lexigram touch pad, which is connected to a computer that displays—while a male voice speaks—the words he selects. But Kanzi's finger slips off
60 the keys. "We're trying to solve this problem," says Savage-Rumbaugh.

She and her colleagues have been testing the bonobos' ability to express their thoughts vocally, rather than by pushing buttons. In one experiment she described to me, she placed Kanzi and Panbanisha, his sister, in separate rooms where they could hear but not see each other. Through lexigrams, Savage-Rumbaugh explained to Kanzi that he would be given yogurt. He was then asked to communicate this information to Panbanisha. "Kanzi vocalized, then Panbanisha vocalized in
70 return and selected 'yogurt' on the keyboard in front of her," Savage-Rumbaugh tells me.

With these and other ape-language experiments, says Savage-Rumbaugh, "the mythology of human uniqueness is coming under challenge. If apes can learn language, which we once thought unique to humans, then it suggests that ability is not innate in just us."

But many linguists[2] argue that these bonobos are simply very skilled at getting what they want, and that their abilities do not constitute language. "I do not believe that there has
80 ever been an example anywhere of a nonhuman expressing an opinion, or asking a question. Not ever," says Geoffrey Pullum, a linguist at the University of California at Santa Cruz. "It would be wonderful if animals could say things about the world, as opposed to just signaling a direct emotional state or need. But they just don't."

---

[2] **linguist** an expert who studies the nature and structure of many languages, and the variations among them

Whatever the dimension of Kanzi's abilities, he and I did manage to communicate. I'd told Savage-Rumbaugh about some of my adventures, and she invited me to perform a Maori war dance. I beat my chest, slapped my thighs and hollered.

90 The bonobos sat quiet and motionless for a few seconds, then all but Kanzi snapped into a frenzy, the noise deafening as they screamed, bared their teeth and pounded on the walls and floor of their enclosure. Still calm, Kanzi waved an arm at Savage-Rumbaugh, as if asking her to come closer, then let loose with a stream of squeaks and squeals. "Kanzi says he knows you're not threatening them," Savage-Rumbaugh said to me," and he'd like you to do it again just for him, in a room out back, so the others won't get upset."

I'm skeptical, but I follow the researcher through the
100 complex, out of Kanzi's sight. I find him, all alone, standing behind protective bars. Seeing me, he slapped his chest and thighs, mimicking my war dance, as if inviting me to perform an encore. I obliged, of course, and Kanzi joined in with gusto.

Discuss and Decide

Which details about the author's interactions with Kanzi suggest that Kanzi communicates beyond "signaling a direct emotional state or need"?

When Animals Communicate, They Are Not Using "Language"

by Mia Lewis

NOTES

Over the years, a number of research studies have shown that it is possible to teach an animal to communicate using sign language or specially designed computer keyboards. Bonobos or other primates raised in captivity and trained from birth may over the course of many years learn signs or symbols representing hundreds of words. They may even be able to string a couple of them together to make basic phrases. Dogs, and even birds, can be trained to recognize and respond to many words and signals.

10   But does any of this constitute the ability to use language? Many linguists, zoologists, and other scientists say no. They believe that the ability to use language is unique to humans. We have something in our brains that enables us to learn and use language in a way that animals never can.

Skeptical scientists insist that when chimpanzees or other animals are taught to use words or signs, more often than not they are simply performing a kind of trick in order to receive a reward—usually food. That is why the animals do not then go on to create more words of their own, or string them together
20   into complex sentences. A human baby, on the other hand, rapidly progresses from saying single words to being able to form complex sentences.

One famous linguist compares the animals that participate in human language studies to Olympic athletes. "Humans can

fly about 30 feet—that's what they do in the Olympics," Noam
Chomsky said in an interview. In other words, just because you
can train a gymnast to fly through the air, that does not mean
humans can fly. Likewise, the chimps in these studies aren't
really using language, and the studies don't tell us anything
30 about actual animal communication. "If higher apes were
incapable of anything beyond the trivialities that have been
shown in these experiments, they would have been extinct
millions of years ago," Dr. Chomsky said.

Of course animals communicate with each other using
various means—sounds, signals, even smells and vibrations.
And as research technologies improve, scientists discover more
and more about the complexity and sophistication of these
communications. But all the same, those communication
methods are not the same as language. They lack one or more
40 of the many attributes that make up human language, such as
the following:

— Displacement: the ability to communicate ideas about
things not present in time or space;

— Discreteness: discrete units of sound being combined to
make up meaning;

— Productivity: the ability to combine the words in a
language to produce an infinite number of meanings.

Even if it isn't "language," the natural communication in
animal species is more interesting and important to study
50 than the tricks they can be taught. After all, what chimpanzees
communicate to each other in the wild—without language—
must go far beyond the 200-300 words they can be taught in a
laboratory setting.

Close Read

What makes animals' natural communication—"sounds, signals, even
smells and vibrations"—less complex than human language?

_____

_____

Source 3: Graphic Feature

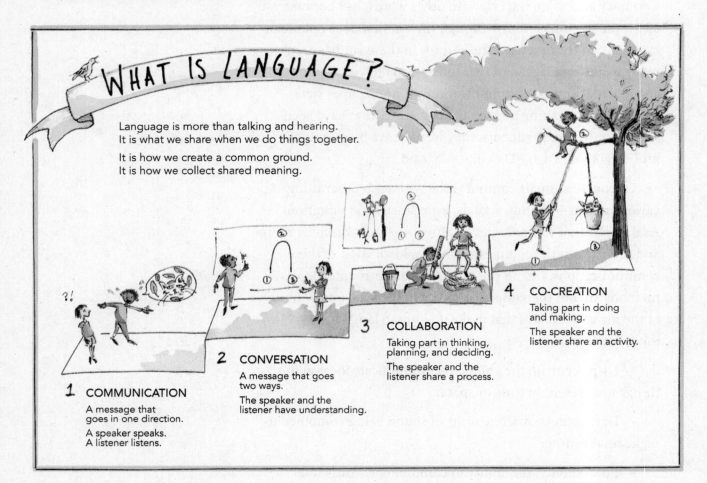

WHAT IS LANGUAGE?

Language is more than talking and hearing.
It is what we share when we do things together.

It is how we create a common ground.
It is how we collect shared meaning.

1 COMMUNICATION
A message that goes in one direction.
A speaker speaks.
A listener listens.

2 CONVERSATION
A message that goes two ways.
The speaker and the listener have understanding.

3 COLLABORATION
Taking part in thinking, planning, and deciding.
The speaker and the listener share a process.

4 CO-CREATION
Taking part in doing and making.
The speaker and the listener share an activity.

Discuss and Decide

How is language different from communication? Cite evidence in your discussion.

Respond to Questions on Step 3 Sources

These questions will help you think about the sources you've read. Use your notes and refer to the sources to answer the questions. Your answers to these questions will help you write your essay.

1 Why did Kanzi become a candidate for learning language?

    a. Sue Savage-Rumbaugh took him from the wild to teach him.

    b. Sue Savage-Rumbaugh had taught all members of Kanzi's family.

    c. He was present when his mother, Matata, was being taught how to communicate.

    d. He was the psychologists' favorite bonobo.

2 According to Source 2, what do the methods animals use to communicate with one another reveal about them?

    a. They show that animals have a language similar to humans.

    b. They show that animals can communicate in many ways that are superior to human language.

    c. They show that animals communicate in ways that are as sophisticated as human language.

    d. They show that humans are not communicating effectively.

3 Which words best support your answer to Question 2?

    a. "...when chimpanzees or other animals are taught to use words or signs, more often than not they are simply performing a kind of trick..."

    b. "But all the same, those communication methods are not the same as language."

    c. "...what chimpanzees communicate to each other in the wild— without language—must go far beyond the 200-300 words they can be taught in a laboratory..."

    d. "They lack one or more of the many attributes that make up human language..."

4 Which best supports the idea that co-creation is the most advanced stage of language?

    a. "It is how we create common ground."

    b. "The speaker and the listener share an activity."

    c. "Language is more than talking and hearing."

    d. "A message that goes two ways."

5 Is the evidence from one source more credible than the evidence from another source? When you evaluate the credibility of a source, consider the expertise of the author and/or the organization responsible for the information. Record your reasons.

Source	Credible?	Reasons
Magazine Article Speaking Bonobo		
Magazine Article When Animals Communicate They Are Not Using "Language"		
Graphic Feature What Is Language?		

6 **Prose Constructed-Response** You have read three texts about animals' ability to learn and use language. Analyze the strengths of the arguments made in at least two of the texts. Cite textual evidence to support your ideas.

_____

_____

_____

_____

_____

_____

_____

_____

_____

_____

_____

Part 2: Write

ASSIGNMENT

You have read about the animals and whether or not they are capable of learning or using language. Now write an argumentative essay explaining why you agree or disagree with the idea that animals can learn and use language. Support your claim with details from what you have read.

Plan

Use the graphic organizer to help you outline the structure of your argumentative essay.

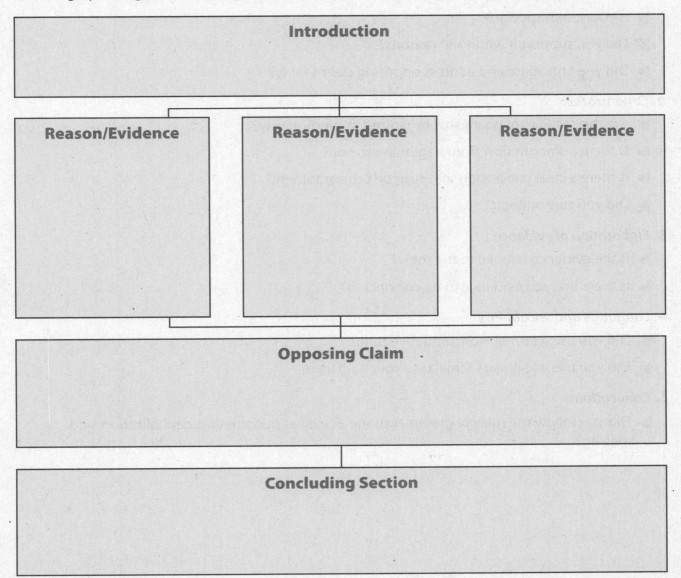

Introduction

Reason/Evidence

Reason/Evidence

Reason/Evidence

Opposing Claim

Concluding Section

Draft

 Use your notes and completed graphic organizer to write a first draft of your argumentative essay.

Revise and Edit

Look back over your essay and compare it to the Evaluation Criteria. Revise your essay and edit it to correct spelling, grammar, and punctuation errors.

Evaluation Criteria

Your teacher will be looking for:

1. Statement of purpose
- ▶ Is your claim specific?
- ▶ Did you support it with valid reasons?
- ▶ Did you anticipate and address opposing claims fairly?

2. Organization
- ▶ Are the sections of your essay organized in a logical way?
- ▶ Is there a smooth flow from beginning to end?
- ▶ Is there a clear conclusion that supports the argument?
- ▶ Did you stay on topic?

3. Elaboration of evidence
- ▶ Is the evidence relative to the topic?
- ▶ Is there enough evidence to be convincing?

4. Language and vocabulary
- ▶ Did you use a formal, noncombative tone?
- ▶ Did you use vocabulary familiar to your audience?

5. Conventions
- ▶ Did you follow the rules of grammar usage as well as punctuation, capitalization, and spelling?

Disaster!

Informative Essay

STEP 1

ANALYZE THE MODEL

Evaluate two informative essays. The first is about the causes of house fires and the second is about a particular house fire.

STEP 2

PRACTICE THE TASK

Write an informative essay that compares and contrasts tornadoes and hurricanes.

STEP 3

PERFORM THE TASK

Write an informative essay that compares and contrasts rogue waves and tsunamis.

An informative essay, also called an expository essay, is a short work of nonfiction that informs and explains. Unlike fiction, nonfiction deals with real people, events, and places without changing any facts. Examples of nonfiction writing include newspapers, magazines, and online articles, as well as biographies, speeches, movie and book reviews, and true-life adventure stories.

The sources in this unit describe actual disasters—fires, hurricanes, and the like. The information in these texts is factual.

IN THIS UNIT, you will evaluate the way writers organized their informative essays and analyze information from nonfiction articles, maps, and data displays. Then you will use what you have learned to write informative essays of your own.

What causes home fires and how can we prevent them?

You will read:

▶ **AN INSTRUCTIONAL ARTICLE**

Organizing Your Writing

You will analyze:

▶ **TWO STUDENT MODELS**

Hunting for Hazards

One Thing Led to Another

Source Materials for Step 1

Ms. Galen's students read the following text below to help them learn strategies for organizing informative essays. As you read, underline information that you find useful.

NOTES

Organizing Your Writing

by Russ Weisman

You probably have already had to complete writing assignments that required you to plan, research, and write an informative essay. Whether the subject is science, history, or another nonfiction topic, you will need to determine the way you will organize your essay before you begin to write.

When you organize an informative essay, you need to first determine how the pieces of information relate to one another. Graphic organizers can help you plan your organizational structure.

Main Ideas and Supporting Details

The success of your informative essay will depend on your main idea and supporting details. In the graphic organizer below, jot down your main idea or central point. Then identify the details you will use to support or explain your main idea.

MAIN IDEA				
Detail	Detail	Detail	Detail	Detail

Cause-and-Effect Organization

Cause-and-effect writing explains why something happened, why something exists, or what resulted from an action or condition. The way a cause-and-effect writing is organized depends on your topic and purpose for writing. Different types of cause-and-effect organization are shown below.

1. Cause-to-Effect Organization

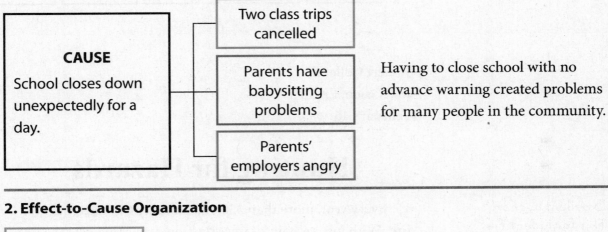

Having to close school with no advance warning created problems for many people in the community.

2. Effect-to-Cause Organization

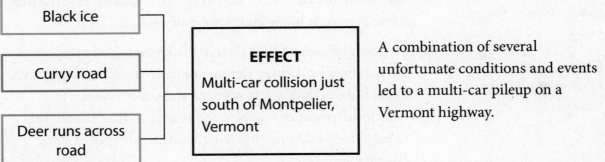

A combination of several unfortunate conditions and events led to a multi-car pileup on a Vermont highway.

3. Causal Chain

In a causal chain, one event causes the next event to occur. The second event causes the third event, which causes the fourth. You may use a causal chain to explain why a series of events took place.

Discuss and Decide

You are going to read two informative essays on home fires. Which pattern of organization seems most appropriate for the topic?

© Houghton Mifflin Harcourt Publishing Company

Analyze Two Student Models for Step 1

Robert organized his informative essay logically. Read his essay closely. The red side notes are comments made by his teacher, Ms. Galen.

Robert's Model

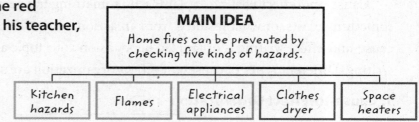

Robert Colleran
Ms. Galen, English
February 16

Hunting for Hazards

Excellent opener! This fact identifies the main idea for your essay.

Every year, more than 350,000 American homes catch on fire. With just an hour of investigation, you can locate the fire hazards in your home and prevent home fires.

Good grouping of topics related to kitchen hazards.

Most household fires start in the kitchen. You can prevent kitchen fires by keeping flammable items away from the stove. Don't leave potholders, cardboard and paper containers, dishcloths, or paper towels near any heat source. In fact, the safest thing to do is to find a permanent, safe spot to store flammables.

Your topic sentence clearly announces the paragraph topic.

Any open flame can cause a home fire. A birthday candle can be knocked over and set table decorations, gifts, paper tablecloths, and napkins on fire. Adults should always be in a room while candles are lit. Make sure that matches, lighters, and candles are out of the reach of children. Fireplaces should be covered by a screen or a grate to prevent sparks from flying onto rugs and to keep logs from tumbling out of the fireplace.

Small electrical appliances such as toasters, steam irons, and curling irons can remain hot after they are turned off. Don't ever put such items away until they have cooled down completely.

Clothes dryers cause many fires every year. Dryers have vents that get filled with lint. When lint builds up, the dryers overheat. The lint and the clothes then become the fuel for a fire. To prevent dryers from overheating, clean out lint vents after every use. In addition, don't overload the dryer.

Fixed and portable space heaters (including wood stoves) cause about one-third of all home-heating fires. When using a heater, keep the area around and above it clear. Keep it out of the way of foot traffic so itcan't get knocked over. Don't leave it on when no one is in the room.

Surprising fact!

You can take other steps to prevent fires in your home. Four of every ten deaths from home fires occur in homes that do not have smoke alarms. So if you don't have a smoke alarm, get one! And then check the batteries regularly. Dead batteries are a huge hazard.

There is one final rule: Everyone living in a home should know the best escape route in case of a fire. Make a plan that works, and decide where to meet once you're outside your house or apartment.

Adding these warnings to the conclusion is an excellent idea. So this paragraph is more than a summary. It may save lives!

Nice work! Your essay has a strong main idea supported by details!

Discuss and Decide

How does the information about clothes dryers relate to Robert's main idea?

Karen organized her informative essay as a causal chain. In addition, Karen's use of narrative description highlights the details of the events she reports. Ms. Galen made her notes in red.

Karen's Model

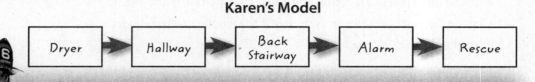

Dryer → Hallway → Back Stairway → Alarm → Rescue

Karen Dayton
Ms. Galen, English
February 16

One Thing Led to Another
A Report on the House Fire at 90 East 35ᵗʰ Street

My next door neighbor's house caught on fire, and four huge fire trucks responded to the alarm. I was able to interview our town's Fire Chief about the causes of this fire. In part, that was thanks to the fact that my dad is the Fire Chief! Also, I interviewed our neighbors, and they took me on a tour of the house so I could get a firsthand look at the damage.

The Source of the Problem. The laundry room of this large, 4-story, 60-year-old brick house is located in the basement. One of the two teenage sons had overloaded the clothes dryer and did not clean out the lint trap. In fact, later interviews with the parents suggest that they were not sure whether cleaning the lint trap had ever been discussed with their sons.

Out of the Laundry Room. The high heat of the dryer caused the lint to catch fire, which then set the clothes on fire. There is a fire alarm in the basement, which is a good thing. There should be a smoke alarm near a heat source. However, the batteries were old, so this alarm was not activated by the smoke and fire, which began to creep out of the laundry room into the hallway outside the door.

Good Intro!

Karen, I like your boldfaced headings! They make your causal chain organization very clear.

The warning about batteries is important. It was a good idea to include it.

I can picture the smoke and fire moving thanks to your description.

Up the Back Stairway. The house has two separate stairways. The back stairway leads directly from the basement, just outside the laundry room, to the first and second floors and to the attic on the house's top (and third) floor. The boys' bedrooms are located on the attic floor. Because hot air rises, the heavy smoke from the fire rose quickly. The three flights of stairs acted as a funnel, allowing the fire to spread into both attic bedrooms.

Good use of descriptive details.

Alarm Finally Sounds! The fire department estimated that the smoke reached the second floor about ten minutes after the fire started in the dryer. Luckily, the batteries *had been replaced* in the smoke alarm on the second floor, so, this alarm sounded both in the house and at the fire station.

Parents Rescue Sons! The alarm wakened the boys' parents. They spotted the thick cloud of smoke moving up the back stairway and rushed upstairs to the attic. Both boys were semiconscious. Their parents dragged them down the stairs and out of the house. Just then, the fire department arrived.

Again, all five of your main paragraphs do a good job of showing how "one thing led to another." (Good Title!)

Fire Chief Dayton stated, "This is exactly the kind of fire that can wipe out an entire family. It is very lucky that we arrived in time. This fire was caused, in part, due to negligence. If the boys knew to clean out the lint trap, there may have been no fire. If the dryer hadn't been overloaded, the heat would not have built up so quickly. If the batteries had been changed in all of the alarms, the Fire Department would have arrived 20 to 30 minutes sooner. That can be the difference between life and death."

The fire chief explains the causal chain in a clear way.

Nice work! Your essay explains the causes and effects of the fire clearly.

Discuss and Decide

Discuss whether the descriptive language added or took away from your understanding of the fire's causes and effects.

Terminology of Informative Essays

Read each term and explanation. Then look back and analyze each student model. Find an example to complete the chart. Finally, make a claim about which model was more successful in illustrating each term.

Term	Explanation	Example from Student Essays
topic	The **topic** is a word or phrase that tells what the essay is about.	
text structure	The **text structure** is the organizational pattern of an essay.	
main idea	The **main idea** is the controlling, or overarching, idea that states the main point the writer chooses to make.	
supporting evidence	The **supporting evidence** is relevant quotations and concrete details that support the main idea.	
domain-specific vocabulary	**Domain-specific vocabulary** is content-specific words that are not generally used in conversation.	
text features	**Text features** are features that help organize the text, such as: headings, boldface type, italic type, bulleted or numbered lists, sidebars, and graphic aids, including charts, tables, timelines, illustrations, and photographs.	

Claim:_____

Support your claim by citing text evidence.

_____

_____

How are hurricanes and tornadoes alike and different?

You will read:

▶ **AN INSTRUCTIONAL ESSAY**
What Is ... Comparison-and-Contrast Organization

▶ **A MAP**
Hurricanes and Tornadoes in the U.S.

▶ **TWO INFORMATIONAL TEXTS**
What You Should Know About Tornadoes

Basic Facts About Hurricanes

You will write:

▶ **AN INFORMATIVE ESSAY**
How are hurricanes and tornadoes alike and different?

Source Materials for Step 2

AS YOU READ You will be writing an informative essay that describes the similarities and differences between hurricanes and tornadoes. Carefully study the sources in Step 2. As you read, underline and circle information that you may cite as textual evidence when you write your essay.

Source 1: Instructional Essay

What Is . . .

Comparison-and-Contrast Organization

by Moira McCarthy

When you write an informative essay, you need to consider your topic and select the best way to organize your information. For instance, if you wanted to examine the reason why a particular event takes place, you might use cause-and-effect organization.

To analyze the similarities and differences between two subjects, you will want to use comparison-and-contrast organization. In the essay you are going to write, you will analyze the similarities and differences between hurricanes and tornadoes. Remember to discuss the same aspects of both: If you discuss the areas affected by hurricanes, you must also remember to discuss the areas affected by tornadoes.

You can refer to the framework on the right for your comparison-and-contrast essay.

Framework for a Comparison-and-Contrast Essay

Introduction
A clear statement of your subjects and your main idea about how they are alike or different

Body
The two or three most important similarities or differences

Conclusion:
Summary of your main idea, noting its importance or usefulness

1. Analyze   2. Practice   3. Perform

Source 2: Map

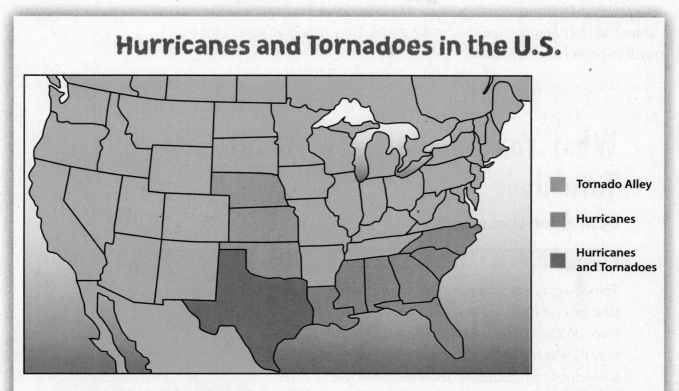

Hurricanes and Tornadoes in the U.S.

Tornado Alley

Hurricanes

Hurricanes and Tornadoes

About 1,300 tornadoes hit the U.S. each year, with a total average cost of $500 million in damages. In an average three-year period, roughly five hurricanes strike the U.S. coastline, causing annual damage of about $15 billion.

Tornadoes

"Tornado Alley" is an informal term that describes the area in the United States where the strongest tornadoes occur most frequently—particularly northern Texas, Oklahoma, Kansas, and Nebraska. Other states greatly affected by tornadoes include Arkansas, Louisiana, Mississippi, Alabama, Tennessee, and Georgia.

Hurricanes

In the United States, communities located in the South Atlantic and Gulf states (Texas, Louisiana, Mississippi, Alabama, and Florida) are the most vulnerable to hurricanes. Residents in these areas are likely to get advanced warnings about approaching hurricanes to allow them to seek shelter before hurricanes strike.

Source 3: Informational Text

AS YOU READ Notice the relationship between the headings and the content of the paragraphs in Sources 3 and 4. They may give you a hint at possible points of comparison.

What You Should Know About Tornadoes

by Sheldon Hammond

SHAPE AND PHYSICAL DESCRIPTION

Tornadoes are rapidly spinning columns of air that extend from the sky and touch the ground. A tornado can be described as *cyclonic* because of the way its winds rotate. In the Northern Hemisphere, tornadoes spin counterclockwise, but in the Southern Hemisphere tornadoes rotate clockwise. Frequently visible as giant cones, the tornado's narrow point may appear to touch the ground while the wider part is at the top of the column.

SIZE VERSUS IMPACT

As you can tell from their cone-like appearance, tornadoes' point of contact with land is relatively small. Most tornadoes are only a few hundred feet across, with winds reaching one hundred miles an hour. They can remain on the ground for miles. Some exceptionally large tornadoes stretch a few miles across, stay on the ground for many miles, and have winds that exceed 300 miles an hour. Some tornadoes can even have more than one point—destroying one house and leaving the next virtually untouched.

PREDICTABILITY PROBLEMS

While meteorologists are able to identify storms that are likely to bring tornadoes with them, there is no way to predict exactly where or if a tornado will make landfall or how powerful its winds will be. It is a tornado's high wind speeds that present a difficult, almost unsolvable problem to residents living in a tornado zone.

WHERE ON EARTH?

Every continent with the exception of Antarctica has been visited by tornadoes. However, the majority of tornadoes occur in North America. They are common throughout the United States, but are most frequent in the region known as "Tornado Alley." "Tornado Alley" is an area of the Great Plains in the central United States where tornadoes are most frequent.

PROTECTING LIFE AND PROPERTY

One reason relatively few people are killed by tornadoes is that they are often visible in the distance. Most people are able to prepare because their visibility sometimes provides sufficient warning to alert local residents to get to a safe location. However, some tornadoes develop rapidly or may be obscured by clouds and rain, making advance warning difficult. An underground cellar or basement is often the safest refuge during a tornado. What's more, very little can be done to protect property from tornadoes. About 1,300 tornadoes hit the U.S. each year, causing damage to hundreds of homes.

Discuss and Decide

Evaluate whether the essay or the map gives you a better understanding of what parts of the United States face tornadoes.

Basic Facts About Hurricanes

by Eve Perry

What Qualifies as a Hurricane?

Hurricanes are among the largest, most powerful storms on Earth. All hurricanes form near the equator because they require warm tropical oceans to get their start. To be classified as a hurricane, the wind from a rotating storm must reach at least 74 miles per hour, though the strongest hurricanes will have winds in excess of 150 miles per hour. In the Northern Hemisphere, the winds rotate counterclockwise. In the Southern Hemisphere, they rotate clockwise.

What Causes a Hurricane?

Typical hurricanes are about 300 miles wide, although they can vary considerably in size. Hurricanes are cyclonic. That is, the winds of a hurricane rotate towards the center of the storm. They are fueled by the evaporation of warm ocean waters. The fastest winds of a hurricane are generally nearest the "eye," though in the eye itself, the wind is often not powerful at all. Hurricanes are always at their strongest in warm seas and with atmospheric conditions that allow the storm to rotate tightly around its eye. Hurricanes can be identified by their heavy rains and strong winds that blow objects around.

1. Analyze   2. Practice   3. Perform

Hurricanes in the U.S.

Many of the hurricanes that strike the United States form near the African coastline before traveling across the Atlantic Ocean. As they move west, they gain strength. Although many large storms form during hurricane season, in a three-year average, only five make landfall in the United States. Each hurricane can cause billions of dollars in damage. Most hurricanes claim few lives in the United States, but Hurricane Katrina killed over 1,000 people in 2005 and caused roughly 100 billion dollars in damage.

Storm Surges

Besides the damage caused by extreme winds and flooding rains, the high winds can create a "storm surge." A storm surge occurs when ocean water is blown by the wind onto the shore. This storm surge raises the level of the ocean, which can then destroy everything in its path by flooding beaches, blowing roofs off houses, toppling buildings, flipping cars, and causing massive trees to tumble to the ground like toothpicks. Out to sea, waves generated by hurricanes can be as high as 70 feet and can create disastrous problems for boats and ships.

Warning Time and Predictability

Fortunately most residents of the U. S. have a lot of warning before a hurricane. Anyone likely to experience hurricanes should make it an absolute practice to listen to instruction from the local government, particularly if officials call for an evacuation. It is also important to make sure that you have enough food and water to last several days in case you lose power. Preparations beforehand can help minimize the fatalities and damage caused by hurricanes, so it is important to make use of this advanced warning.

Discuss and Decide

What are three possible points of comparison between tornadoes or hurricanes? Cite text evidence in your response.

Respond to Questions on Step 2 Sources

The following questions will help you think about the sources you've read.
Use your notes and refer to the sources as you answer the questions. Your
answers will help you write your essay.

1 What makes tornadoes cyclonic?
   a. the speed of the winds
   b. the size of the base
   c. the way their winds rotate
   d. the length of the winds

2 Why do U.S. residents get more advance warning for a hurricane than
they do for a tornado?
   a. There is better technology for predicting hurricanes.
   b. Hurricanes form before they travel across the Atlantic Ocean.
   c. Hurricanes cause more damage and need more monitoring.
   d. Hurricanes don't occur as often as tornadoes.

3 Based on the information in Source 2, which of the following statements
is true?
   a. More tornadoes than hurricanes hit the U.S. each year, and these
      tornadoes cause greater financial damage than do hurricanes.
   b. More hurricanes than tornadoes hit the U.S. each year, and these
      hurricanes cause greater financial damage than do tornadoes.
   c. Although far more tornadoes than hurricanes hit the U.S. each year,
      the financial cost of hurricane damage is far greater than the cost of
      tornado damage.
   d. Although far more hurricanes than tornadoes hit the U.S. each year,
      the financial cost of tornado damage is far greater than the cost of
      hurricane damage.

1. Analyze   2. Practice   3. Perform

4 Why do storm surges occur?

   a. Ocean water is blown on shore by high winds.

   b. Wind rotates very quickly to form a cyclone of water.

   c. Earth shakes and causes the water level of the ocean to rise.

   d. Excessive rain raises the level of the ocean.

5 Which words below best describe the dangers of storm surges?

   a. "Hurricanes are very large wind and rainstorms."

   b. "Out to sea, waves generated by hurricanes can be as high as 70 feet and can create disastrous problems for boats and ships."

   c. ". . . always at their strongest in shallow warm seas and with atmospheric conditions that allow the storm to rotate tightly around its eye."

   d. ". . . flooding beaches, by blowing roofs off houses, toppling buildings, flipping cars, and causing massive trees to tumble to the ground . . ."

6 **Prose Constructed-Response** What is the main idea of the section "Size Versus Impact" in Source 3? Be sure to state the main idea, as well as its supporting details. Cite text evidence in your response.

_____

_____

_____

_____

7 **Prose Constructed-Response** Look again at the map in Source 2 and the text in Source 4. Which source gave you a better understanding about how hurricanes form? Cite text evidence in your response.

_____

_____

_____

_____

Write an informative essay to answer the
question: In what ways are hurricanes and
tornadoes alike and different?

Planning and Prewriting

Before you start writing, review your sources and determine the key points
and supporting details to include in your essay. As you evaluate each point,
collect textual evidence in the chart below.

 You may prefer to do your planning on a computer.

Decide on Key Points

Characteristics	Tornadoes	Hurricanes
1. **Appearance** ☐ Alike ☑ Different	Cone-shaped	Heavy rains and winds
2. **Frequency in U.S.** ☐ Alike ☐ Different		
3. **Location in U.S.** ☐ Alike ☐ Different		
4. **Casualties** ☐ Alike ☐ Different		
5. **Cost and Damage** ☐ Alike ☐ Different		

Developing Your Topic

Before you write your essay, decide how you want to arrange your ideas. You can use one of the patterns of organization described below or come up with you own arrangement—whatever works best for your subject. Your essay will begin with an introductory paragraph and end with a concluding paragraph.

Point-by-Point Discuss the first point of comparison or contrast for both tornadoes and hurricanes, then move on to the second point. If you choose this organization, you will read across the rows of this chart.

Topic	Tornadoes	Hurricanes	
1. Appearance		→	If you use this organizational structure, your essay will have a paragraph comparing or contrasting warning times for tornadoes and hurricanes followed by paragraphs comparing and contrasting the other points in your chart.
2. Frequency in U.S.		→	
3. Location in U.S.		→	
4. Casualties		→	
5. Cost and Damage		→	

Subject-by-Subject Discuss all the points about tornadoes before moving on to hurricanes. If you choose this method, you will be reading across the rows of this chart.

Topic	Appearance	Frequency in U.S.	Location in U.S.	Casualties	Cost and Damage
1. Tornadoes					→
2. Hurricanes					→

If you use this organizational structure, your essay will have one or two paragraphs addressing all your points as they relate to tornadoes, followed by one or two paragraphs addressing all your points as they relate to hurricanes.

Finalize Your Plan

Use your responses and notes from previous pages to create a detailed plan for your essay. Fill in the chart below.

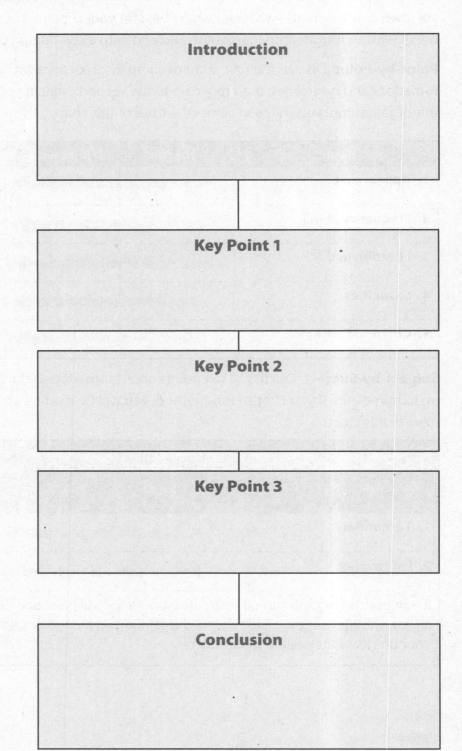

▶ Introduce your topic and "hook" your audience with an interesting detail, question, or quotation.

▶ Follow a framework like the one shown here to organize your main ideas and supporting evidence.

▶ Include relevant facts, concrete details, and other textual evidence to support your points of comparison.

▶ Summarize the key points and restate your main idea.

▶ Include an insight that supports your main idea.

Introduction

Key Point 1

Key Point 2

Key Point 3

Conclusion

Draft Your Essay

As you write, think about:

▶ **Audience:** Your teacher

▶ **Purpose:** Demonstrate your understanding of the specific requirements of an informative essay.

▶ **Style:** Use a formal and objective tone.

▶ **Transitions:** Use words and phrases such as *for example* or *because* to create cohesion, or flow.

Revise

Revision Checklist: Self Evaluation

Use the checklist below to guide your analysis.

 If you drafted your essay on the computer, you may wish to print it out so that you can more easily evaluate it.

Ask Yourself	Tips	Revision Strategies
1. Does the introduction grab the audience's attention?	Underline sentences in the introduction that engage the readers.	Add an interesting question, fact, or observation to get the reader's attention.
2. Is each point of comparison supported by textual evidence, facts, and concrete details?	Circle textual evidence.	Add textual evidence, if necessary.
3. Are appropriate and varied transitions used to connect and contrast ideas?	Place a checkmark next to each transitional word or phrase.	Add transitional words or phrases where needed to clarify the relationships between ideas.
4. Does the concluding section sum up key ideas? Does it give the audience something to think about?	Double underline the summary of key points in the concluding section. Underline the insight offered to readers.	Add an overarching view of key points or a final observation about the significance of the comparison and contrast.

Revision Checklist: Peer Review

Exchange your essay with a classmate, or read it aloud to your partner. As you read and comment on your classmate's essay, focus on how clearly tornadoes and hurricanes have been compared and contrasted. Help each other identify parts of the drafts that need strengthening, reworking, or even a complete new approach.

What To Look For	Notes for My Partner
1. Does the introduction grab the audience's attention?	
2. Is it clear what topics are being compared and contrasted?	
3. Is each point of comparison supported by well-chosen and sufficient textual evidence, including facts and concrete details?	
4. Are appropriate and varied transitions used to connect and contrast ideas?	
5. Does the concluding section sum up key ideas? Does it give the reader something to think about?	

Edit

Edit your essay to correct spelling, grammar, and punctuation errors..

STEP
3
PERFORM THE TASK

How are rogue waves and tsunamis alike and different?

You will read:

▶ **TWO INFORMATIONAL TEXTS**
What Are Rogue Waves?

What Causes Tsunamis?

You will write:

▶ **AN INFORMATIVE ESSAY**
How are rogue waves and tsunamis alike and different?

What Are Rogue Waves?

by Neveah Simmons

A rogue wave is not just a big wave. A rogue wave is an enormous wave that occurs far out in the ocean. Rogue waves are also known as "freak" waves because they seem to come from nowhere, and no one can predict when or where they will strike. The surrounding sea can appear calm when suddenly a wave as high as 100 feet above the ocean's surface comes crashing towards you. That's as high as a ten-story building. So just imagine your terror if you witnessed a wall of water this high headed relentlessly toward your boat

10 or ship?

What We Know–and Don't Know

Rogue waves are rare in the parts of the ocean that humans visit. This fact makes them difficult to study. Because they cannot be predicted in advance, scientists and their instruments are rarely in the right place at the right time with the right equipment to collect data about rogue waves. Although rogue waves are sometimes described as "random" waves, that description is probably *not* accurate. If it were true, we would have to conclude that rogue waves happen without a single, clear-cut pattern. There probably are patterns, but they

20 have not been discovered yet.

WHY SO HIGH? What causes these rogue waves to be so high? Scientists don't know for sure, but they do have theories. Many factors affect a wave's height, including wind strength, ocean depth, ocean currents, and the presence of islands and other obstacles. In fact, some other types of waves *can* reach the same height as rogue waves, but they are generally predictable and more avoidable than rogue waves. For instance, in the midst of a hurricane, wind-driven waves can be just as high as rogue waves.

30 **SPOTTING A ROGUE WAVE** The defining feature of a rogue wave is not just that it is so huge, but that *it does not match the surrounding ocean conditions*. To identify a rogue wave, pay attention to the direction of the prevailing wave patterns. A wave coming from a different direction is quite possibly a rogue wave.

A LIKELY CAUSE Rogue waves seem especially likely to occur in places in the oceans where currents collide. Think of a current as a river in the ocean. There are major currents whose courses can be traced almost all the way around the world. Smaller currents that are affected by local conditions also

40 exist. When one current collides with another current flowing in the opposite direction, a wall of water can build up into an enormous rogue wave.

THE BERMUDA TRIANGLE You may have heard of the infamous "Bermuda Triangle." Some ships have vanished in this mysterious part of the ocean on clear days with no storms in sight. Ocean currents may be responsible. A strong current known as the Gulf Stream runs through the Bermuda Triangle. This current then moves north through the Atlantic Ocean, along the East Coast of the United States. It is possible that the

50 collision of the Gulf Stream currents with other more localized currents provides the clue to unlocking the secret of the Bermuda Triangle and the origin of some rogue waves.

Discuss and Decide

What information about the Bermuda Triangle hints at an explanation of the origin of rogue waves? Cite text evidence in your discussion.

Other Contributing Causes

WIND While it is not believed that wind alone can cause a rogue wave, wind can play a major role in creating rogue waves. The stronger the wind, the higher surface waves tend to be. These strong winds push in the opposite direction against an ocean current, and the collision of the two can create large surface waves.

OCEAN DEPTH The depth of the ocean is also a key factor in creating rogue waves. Rogue waves tend to occur only in deeper water. In order to get high enough to be considered a rogue wave, a lot of water must build up. Very shallow parts of the ocean don't have enough water to create rogue waves. Note that
60   other forms of horribly destructive waves do occur in shallow water. Tsunamis and storm surges are examples, but both are caused by known factors.

ISLANDS AND COASTLINES Geographical features such as islands, or shoals can interrupt and redirect ocean currents. Rogue waves occur most frequently downwind of these geographical features, where smaller waves can overlap and combine. If the waves meet at just the right time, small waves may join with other waves at a single point of focus that allows them to combine into a very large single wave.

70   **WHAT CAN BE DONE TO PREPARE FOR ROGUE WAVES?** Fortunately, rogue waves are very rare and happen only at a reasonable distance from shore. However, if you are out to sea on a boat, it is always a good idea to make sure you are familiar with evacuation plans, the location of life preservers, and other safety equipment.

Close Read

How is a storm surge different from a rogue wave? Cite text evidence in your response.

_____

_____

Source 2: Informational Text

What Causes Tsunamis?

by Jane Sanborn

NOTES

Most waves occur at or near the surface of the ocean. Tsunamis, on the other hand, have their origins at greater depths of the ocean. As a result of the depth of the water, tsunamis can be much more devastating than most surface waves. The reason? Tsunamis move much more water.

Unlike the rogue wave, which is a single wave that is up to 100 feet high, a tsunami is a series of waves. Tsunamis are caused by landslides, volcanoes, or earthquakes that occur on the ocean floor. Large meteorites can also trigger a tsunami if

10 they strike the ocean's surface.

The word "tsunami" is derived from a Japanese word that means "harbor wave." An earthquake that registered 9.0 devastated Japan on March 11, 2011. The resulting tsunami had wave heights of 131 feet and six miles across the land.

What is the most likely cause of a tsunami?

Most tsunamis are triggered by earthquakes that are under the surface of the oceans or close to the coastline. An earthquake is caused when tectonic plates (large pieces of Earth's crust), quickly slide past one another, releasing a huge amount of pent-up energy. Earth's movement during the quake

20 triggers the reaction. Tsunamis are usually characterized by a series of very large waves, rather than a single wave.

When the sea floor becomes shallow near shore, all the water in motion that is traveling the entire height of the water column is suddenly pushed up. (A water column is the expanse between the ocean floor and its surface.) The resulting tsunami floods the shore. Most of the damage of a tsunami is done on land.

Where do tsunamis occur?

Tsunamis are most likely to occur on lands surrounding the Pacific Ocean. That is the western coastline of North and South 30 America, the Aleutian Chain, and the eastern coastline of Asia to Japan. This region is called the "Ring of Fire."

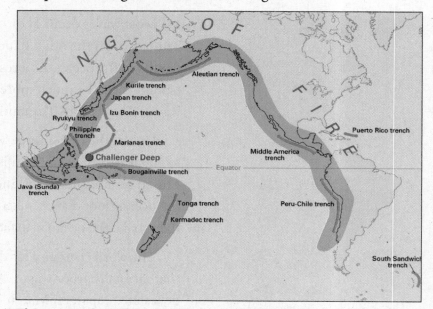

This map identifies the "Ring of Fire," where tsunamis are most likely to occur.

The Ring of Fire

Many warning systems give Pacific populations advance notice of tsunamis. Warning centers combine earthquake data with sea level data. This combined information allows authorities to predict a tsunami path and order evacuation.

Discuss and Decide

Can a rogue wave ever be considered a tsunami? Why or why not? Cite text evidence in your response.

Respond to Questions on Step 3 Sources

The following questions will help you think about the sources you've read. Use your notes and refer to the sources as you answer the questions. Your answers will help you write your essay.

1 What is the main reason that little is known about rogue waves?

   a. They occur in places where humans, including scientists, rarely visit.

   b. It is impossible to distinguish rogue waves from other waves.

   c. Rogue waves do not match the surrounding ocean conditions.

   d. Scientists have little interest in rogue waves because they are rare.

2 Which words best support your answer to Question 1?

   a. "Although rogue waves are sometimes described as 'random' waves, that description is probably not accurate."

   b. "When one current collides with another current flowing in the opposite direction, a wall of water can build up into an enormous rogue wave."

   c. "What makes rogue waves unique is that these 'freak' waves can appear on calm seas!"

   d. "Additionally, rogue waves are rare in the parts of the oceans that humans visit."

3 What is the best meaning for *pent-up* as it is used in "What Causes Tsunamis?"

   a. hot

   b. stored

   c. dangerous

   d. unnatural

4 Which of the following is *not* a claim you could make after reading the sources?

   a. Tsunamis move more water than rogue waves.

   b. There is no way to predict a rogue wave, but there can be an advance warning for a tsunami.

   c. Tsunamis cause the most damage on land.

   d. Rogue waves cause tsunamis.

5 Prose Constructed-Response How do earthquakes and landslides trigger tsunamis? Use details from "What Causes Tsunamis?" in your response.

_____

_____

_____

6 Prose Constructed-Response What is the main idea of the section "Why So High?" in Source 1? Be sure to include its supporting details. Cite text evidence in your response.

_____

_____

_____

7 Prose Constructed-Response How is the Bermuda Triangle important to rogue waves? Cite text evidence in your response.

_____

_____

_____

Part 2: Write

You have read about rogue waves and tsunamis. Write an informative essay comparing and contrasting these two wave events. Cite text evidence from what you have read and viewed.

Plan

Use the graphic organizer to help you outline the structure of your informative essay.

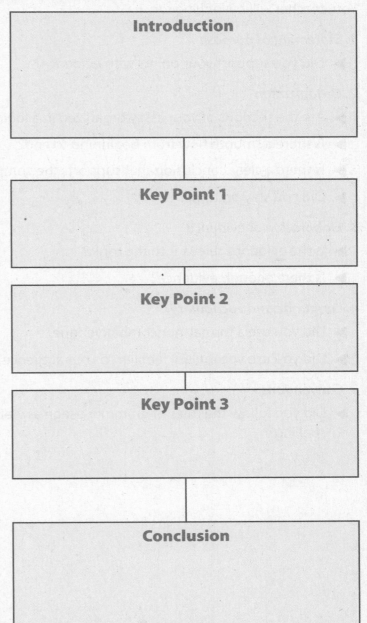

▶ Hook your audience with an interesting detail, question, or quotation.

▶ Identify what you will be comparing and contrasting and state your main idea.

▶ Chose the text structure: **Point-by-Point** Compare and contrast both subjects, one point at a time; or **Subject by Subject** Discuss all the points relating to the first subject before moving on to the second.

▶ Include relevant facts, concrete details, and other evidence.

▶ Summarize the key points and restate your main idea.

▶ Include an insight that follows from and supports your main idea.

Introduction

Key Point 1

Key Point 2

Key Point 3

Conclusion

Draft

 Use your notes and completed graphic organizer to write a first draft of your essay.

Revise and Edit

Look back over your essay and compare it to the Evaluation Criteria. Revise your essay and edit it to correct spelling, grammar, and punctuation errors.

Evaluation Criteria

Your teacher will be looking for:

1. *Statement of purpose*

▶ Did you support your points with evidence?

2. *Organization*

▶ Are the sections of your essay organized in a logical way?

▶ Is there a smooth flow from beginning to end?

▶ Is there a clear conclusion that supports the comparisons?

▶ Did you stay on topic?

3. *Elaboration of evidence*

▶ Is the evidence relevant to the topic?

▶ Is there enough evidence?

4. *Language and vocabulary*

▶ Did you use a formal, noncombative tone?

▶ Did you use vocabulary familiar to your audience?

5. *Conventions*

▶ Did you follow the rules of grammar usage as well as punctuation, capitalization, and spelling?

Viewpoints

Literary Analysis

STEP 1

ANALYZE THE MODEL

Evaluate an analysis of two poems with the same title, "Earth."

STEP 2

PRACTICE THE TASK

Write a literary analysis comparing and contrasting "Six Men and an Elephant" and "The Red and Blue Coat."

STEP 3

PERFORM THE TASK

Write an analysis of how the author of "The White Umbrella" develops the theme of the story.

Why do people love literature—texts that are pure products of the imagination? Perhaps it's because literature shows us something important about life. Literature may not be based on facts, but what it reveals is truth.

At its best, literature draws you into the world of its narrator or characters. Through literature, you can understand characters' feelings and see why they do the things that they do. You may not always agree with their perspective, but you will often understand it.

To use an example that you may be familiar with, Mark Twain's *The Adventures of Tom Sawyer* shows you how people in a small town in Missouri in the mid-1800s thought and felt. You might relate to the way Tom feels about school in some way. Through these similar feelings and attitudes you will begin to understand universal meanings and themes.

IN THIS UNIT, you will evaluate another student's analysis of two poems, both named "Earth." Then you will write a literary analysis of two folk tales. Finally, you will read a short story and write about how the author develops a theme.

ANALYZE THE MODEL

How do others view us?

You will read:
▶ **TWO POEMS**
"Earth"

"Earth"

You will analyze:
▶ **A STUDENT MODEL**
As Earth and Our Ideas Explode

Source Materials for Step 1

Ms. Diaz assigned these two poems to her class to read and analyze. The notes in the side columns were written by David Yuan, a student in Ms. Diaz's class.

Earth

by John Hall Wheelock

Why does the narrator say this "drily"?

"Martian" — an unusual character

"intelligent"? Ironic

"A planet doesn't explode of
   itself," said drily
The Martian astronomer,
   gazing off into the air—
"That they were able to do it
   is proof that highly
intelligent beings must have
   been living there."

1. Analyze   2. Practice   3. Perform

EaRTH

by Oliver Herford

If this little world to-night

    Suddenly should fall thro' space

In a hissing, headlong flight,

    Shrivelling from off its face,

5 As it falls into the sun,

    In an instant every trace

Of the little crawling things—

    Ants, philosophers, and lice,

Cattle, cockroaches, and kings,

10   Beggars, millionaires, and mice,

Men and maggots all as one

    As it falls into the sun—

Who can say but at the same

    Instant from some planet far

15 A child may watch us and exclaim:

    "See the pretty shooting star!"

Earth destroyed—a tragic event

"ants, philosophers"; "cockroaches, and kings"—everything seems equally insignificant

"pretty shooting star"—a tragedy for people on Earth is a beautiful event to an outsider

Irony again

Discuss and Decide

Review David's notes in the side column. Why is the ending of each of these poems ironic?

Analyze a Student Model for Step 1

Read David's literary analysis closely. The red side notes are the comments that his teacher, Ms. Diaz, wrote.

David Yuan
Ms. Diaz, English
February 11

As Earth and Our Ideas Explode

David, great job in comparing and contrasting the two poems!

Nice comparison-contrast of the readers' expectations and the creatures' view of events.

"Earth" by John Hall Wheelock and "Earth" by Oliver Herford are two poems about the end of Earth. Each poem describes this event as seen by creatures from other planets. Although the topics are the same, each creature views the event differently. A happy child sees a "pretty shooting star." A scientist jokes about the "intelligence" humans needed to destroy themselves. However, both poems are similar because they view the end of Earth from an outsider's perspective.

In John Hall Wheelock's poem, a Martian "drily" says that humans have destroyed their planet. He or she does not think of the tragedy or the loss of life, as you or I would. Instead, the end of the world is a chance to be witty. "Intelligence" ended Earth, says the astronomer without sadness.

In Oliver Herford's poem, on the other hand, the end of Earth makes all things equal. Cockroaches and kings become the same. We earthlings may be upset by this, but to the child who sees Earth exploding from far off, our end is a pretty thing. The child's statement in lines 15–16 is ironic: Who would expect the destruction of a planet to be pretty?

Both John Hall Wheelock's "Earth" and Oliver Herford's "Earth" are poems that view Earth's destruction through the eyes of a creature from another planet. In both poems, the creatures do not respond as we would, with pain and sadness. The creatures' responses to Earth's destruction are surprising to us because they are so different from ours.

Give a few more examples of the contrast between the two poems.

Nice conclusion. I like the comparison of the poems and how you show that they are similar. You tie things up well.

Good job, David!

Discuss and Decide

How is the view of the Earth's destruction in the poems different from what you might expect? Cite text evidence in your discussion.

Terminology of Literary Analysis

Read each term and explanation. Then look back at David Yuan's literary analysis and find an example to complete the chart.

Term	Explanation	Example from David's Essay
plot	The **plot** is the series of events in a work of literature.	
character	A **character** is a person, animal, or imaginary creature who takes part in the action of a work of literature.	
theme	The **theme** is the underlying message about life or human nature that the writer wants the reader to understand.	
tone	The **tone** is the attitude the writer takes toward a subject.	
figurative language	**Figurative language** is language used in an imaginative way to express ideas that are not literally true.	
style	**Style** is the particular way in which a work of literature is written—not *what* is said but *how* it is said.	
irony	**Irony** is a contrast between what is expected and what actually happens.	

How does the information we have affect our viewpoint?

You will read:

▶ **AN INFORMATIONAL TEXT**
What Is a. . . Folk Tale

▶ **TWO FOLK TALES**
"Six Men and an Elephant"

"The Red and Blue Coat"

You will write:

▶ **A LITERARY ANALYSIS**
How are the lessons taught by the folk tales alike, and how are they different?

Source Materials for Step 2

AS YOU READ You will be writing a literary analysis about the lessons taught by the folk tales "Six Men and an Elephant" and "The Red and Blue Coat." You will discuss how the lessons are alike and how they are different. Carefully study the sources in Step 2. As you read, underline and circle information that may be useful to you when you write your essay.

Source 1: Informational Text

Folk Tale

by Sandra Merrick

Until folk tales are written down, they are a major part of the oral, or spoken, traditions of a common people. A folk tale is entertaining and meaningful enough to be remembered and shared by generation after generation.

Traveling Tales

Folk tales are the kinds of stories told to children at bedtime and around the fire late at night after the family's work is done. They travel from one culture to another with great ease. The basic story line of one folk tale will often turn up in another culture thousands of miles away.

In West Africa, for example, we find the stories of Anansi the spider. Anansi is both a spider and a human being. He originated from the Akan people of Ghana, where children still love tales of his greed and trickery. Anansi always tries to outwit those who are bigger and stronger.

The People of Folk Tales

The characters in folk tales, although they may have fantastic adventures and may even have magic powers, are ordinary compared to the characters in stories like myths. This may be because they reflect the people who told the tales. The heroes of the African folk tales told in America were often tricksters, characters who used their wits to overcome those who were stronger than they, but not nearly as clever. Folk tales in Europe may feature kings and queens interacting with peasants.

Lessons in Folk Tales

Folk tales usually teach a wise lesson or message about life. This lesson is usually reflected in the behavior of the characters. Consider this tale which is told in cultures around the world:

> A visitor comes to a house. He is poor and in rags, and he asks the homeowners for shelter and food. Many refuse him, and shut their doors against him. Little do they know that the poor visitor is actually a powerful king. He is testing the people to see who is kind and who is heartless.

This folk tale teaches it is important to be kind to people regardless of their appearance. This lesson is conveyed through the main events and the way characters behave and change over the course of the story. Pay attention to the main events and the way characters behave in the two folk tales that follow.

Discuss and Decide

Which actions in the folk tale about the mysterious visitor convey the lesson that it is important to be kind to people? Cite specific evidence from the text in your discussion.

Source 2: Folk Tale

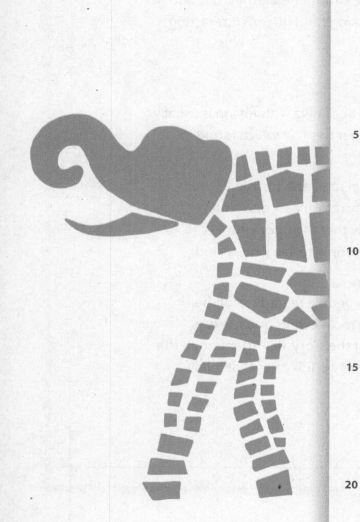

Six Men and an Elephant

a traditional Indian folk tale
retold by John Godfrey Saxe

It was six men of India
     To learning much inclined,
Who went to see the elephant
     (Though all of them were blind),
5 That each by observation
     Might satisfy his mind.

The *first* approached the elephant,
     And happening to fall
Against his broad and sturdy side,
10   At once began to bawl:
"Bless me! but the elephant
     Is very like a wall!"

The *second*, feeling of the tusk,
     Cried, "Ho! what have we here
15 So very round and smooth and sharp?
     To me 'tis mighty clear
This wonder of an elephant
     Is very like a spear!"

The *third* approached the animal,
20   And happening to take
The squirming trunk within his hands,
     Thus boldly up and spake:
"I see," quoth he, "the elephant
     Is very like a snake!"

25 The *fourth* reached out his eager hand,
        And felt about the knee.
    "What most this wondrous beast is like
        Is mighty plain," quoth he;
    "'Tis clear enough the elephant
30   Is very like a tree!"

    The *fifth*, who chanced to touch the ear,
        Said: "E'en the blindest man
    Can tell what this resembles most;
        Deny the fact who can,
35 This marvel of an elephant
        Is very like a fan!"

    The *sixth* no sooner had begun
        About the beast to grope,
    Than, seizing on the swinging tail
40   That fell within his scope,
    "I see," quoth he, "the elephant
        Is very like a rope!"

    And so these men of India
        Disputed loud and long,
45 Each in his own opinion
        Exceeding stiff and strong,
    Though each was partly in the right,
        And all were in the wrong!

Discuss and Decide

With a small group, discuss why all of the men are "in the wrong."
Support your reasons with specific evidence from the text.

THE RED AND BLUE COAT

an African folk tale

There once were two childhood friends who were determined to remain close companions always. When they were grown, they each married and built their houses facing one another. Just a small path formed a border between their farms.

One day a trickster from the village decided to test their friendship. He dressed himself in a two-color coat that was divided down the middle, red on the right side and blue on the left side. Wearing this coat, the man walked along the narrow path between the two houses. The two friends were each working opposite each other in their fields. The trickster made
10 enough noise as he traveled between them to cause each friend to look up from his side of the path at the same moment and notice him.

At the end of the day, one friend said to the other, "Wasn't that a beautiful red coat that man was wearing today?"

"No," replied the other. "It was blue."

"I saw that man clearly as he walked between us!" said the first. "His coat was red."

"You are wrong!" the second man said. "I saw it, too. It was blue."

"I know what I saw!" insisted the first man.
20 "The coat was red."

1. Analyze   2. Practice   3. Perform

"You don't know anything," replied the second angrily. "It was blue!"

"So," shouted the first, "you think I am stupid? I know what I saw. It was red!"

"Blue!" the other man said.

"Red!" "Blue!" "Red!" "Blue!"

They began to beat each other and roll around on the ground.

Just then the trickster returned and faced the two men, who were punching and kicking each other and shouting, "Our friendship is over!"

30 The trickster walked directly in front of them, displaying his coat. He laughed loudly at their silly fight. The two friends saw that his two-color coat was divided down the middle, blue on the left and red on the right.

The two friends stopped fighting and screamed at the man in the two-colored coat, "We have lived side by side all our lives like brothers! It is all *your* fault that we are fighting! You started a war between us."

"Don't blame me for the battle," replied the trickster. "I did not *make* you fight. *Both* of you are wrong. And *both* of you are right. Yes, what each one said was true! You are fighting because you only looked at my coat from your *own* point of view."

Discuss and Decide

With a small group, discuss why each of the friends has a different view of the coat. Cite specific evidence from the text in your discussion.

Respond to Questions on Step 2 Sources

In Step 2, you have read an informative text about folk tales, a traditional Indian folk tale, and an African folk tale. Use your notes and refer to the sources as you answer the questions. Your answers to will help you write your essay.

1. Why does the friendship between the childhood friends in "The Red and Blue Coat" come to an end?
   a. Each friend wants to wear the coat.
   b. A trickster tells lies to one friend about the coat.
   c. The friends disagree about the color of the coat.
   d. One friend steals the coat from another friend.

2. In what way are the childhood friends in "The Red and Blue Coat" different from the blind men in "Six Men and an Elephant"?
   a. The childhood friends are not as curious as the blind men.
   b. The childhood friends have stronger opinions than the blind men.
   c. The childhood friends have the truth revealed to them while the blind men do not.
   d. The childhood friends are more foolish than the blind men.

3. Which of the following best summarizes the common lesson of both "Six Men and an Elephant" and "The Red and Blue Coat"?
   a. People may have incorrect beliefs due to limited information.
   b. Good friends can fight even when they like the same things.
   c. If you ask for what you want, you are more likely to get it.
   d. Some people do not know how to handle new knowledge.

4 **Prose Constructed-Response** Why do each of the blind men in "Six Men and an Elephant" think differently about the elephant? Cite evidence from the poem.

_____

_____

_____

_____

_____

5 **Prose Constructed-Response** How are the reactions of the blind men in "Six Men and an Elephant" and of the boys in "The Red and Blue Coat" similar? Cite evidence from the folk tales in your answer.

_____

_____

_____

_____

_____

6 **Prose Constructed-Response** What do the folk tales tell you about the way characters perceive events? Explain whether someone's viewpoint can ever be completely wrong or completely right. Cite text evidence in your response.

_____

_____

_____

_____

_____

Write a literary analysis that answers the question:
How are the lessons in the folk tales "Six Men and an Elephant" and "The Red and Blue Coat" alike, and how are they different?

Planning and Prewriting

Before you start writing, review your sources and determine the main points and supporting details to include in your essay. As you evaluate each point, collect textual evidence in the chart below.

 You may prefer to do your planning on a computer.

Decide on Key Points

Point	Six Men and an Elephant	The Red and Blue Coat
1. **Main events** ☐ Alike ☑ Different	Blind men try to discover for themselves what an elephant is like.	Childhood friends are fooled by a trickster who plays with the way they see things.
2. **Characters** ☐ Alike ☐ Different		
3. **Characters' actions** ☐ Alike ☐ Different		
4. **Change in characters** ☐ Alike ☐ Different		
5. **Lessons learned from folk tale** ☐ Alike ☐ Different		

1. Analyze   2. Practice   3. Perform

Developing Your Topic

Before you write your essay, decide how you want to arrange your ideas. You can use one of the patterns of organizing described below or come up with you own arrangement—whatever works best for your subject. Your essay will begin with an introductory paragraph and end with a concluding paragraph.

Point-by-Point Discuss the first point of comparison or contrast for both folk tales. Then move on to the second point. If you choose this organization, you will read across the rows of this chart.

Point	Six Men and an Elephant	The Red and Blue Coat	
1. **Main events**			If you use this organizational pattern, your essay will have a paragraph comparing or contrasting the main events in both folk tales, followed by paragraphs comparing and contrasting the other points in your chart.
2. **Characters**			
3. **Characters' actions**			
4. **Change in characters**			
5. **Lessons learned from folk tale**			

Subject-by-Subject Discuss all the points about "Six Men and an Elephant" before moving on to "The Red and Blue Coat." If you choose this method, you will read across the rows of this chart.

Selection	Main events	Characters	Characters' actions	Change in characters	Lessons learned from folk tale
1. **Six Men and an Elephant**					
2. **The Red and Blue Coat**					

If you use this organizational pattern, your essay will have one or two paragraphs addressing all your points related to "Six Men and an Elephant," followed by one or two paragraphs addressing all your points as they relate to "The Red and Blue Coat."

Finalize Your Plan

Use your responses and notes from previous pages to create a detailed plan for your essay. Fill in the chart below.

▶ "Hook" your audience with an interesting detail, question, or quotation.

▶ Follow a framework like the one shown here to organize your main ideas and supporting evidence.

▶ Include relevant facts, concrete details, and other text evidence.

▶ Summarize the key points and restate your main idea.

▶ Include an insight that follows from and supports your main idea.

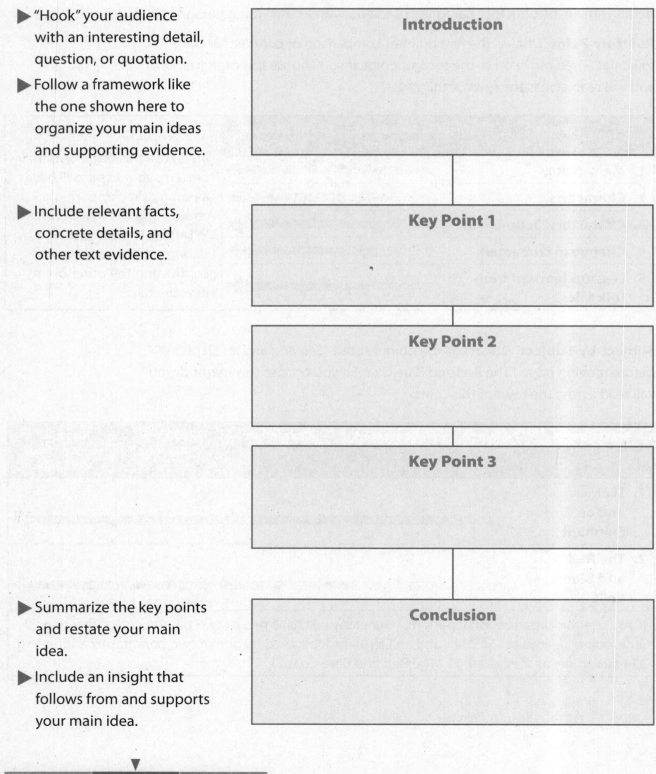

Draft Your Essay

▶ **Audience:** Your teacher

▶ **Purpose:** Demonstrate your understanding of the requirements of a literary analysis.

▶ **Style:** Use a formal and objective tone.

▶ **Transitions:** Use words and phrases such as *also, like,* and *in the same way,* to show similarities and words and phrases such as *but, however, while, unlike,* and *on the other hand,* to show differences.

Revise

Revision Checklist: Self Evaluation

Use the checklist below to guide your analysis.

 If you drafted your essay on the computer, you may wish to print it out so that you can more easily evaluate it.

Ask Yourself	Tips	Revision Strategies
1. Does the introduction "grab" the audience and state your main idea?	Draw a line under the attention-grabbing text. Circle the main idea.	Add an interesting question or fact. Clearly state your main idea.
2. Is each point of comparison supported by evidence, including facts and details from the text?	Circle the specific evidence from the text and draw a line to the point of comparison or contrast it supports.	Add specific evidence from the text, where needed.
3. Are appropriate and varied transitions used to connect, compare, and contrast ideas?	Place a checkmark next to each transitional word or phrase.	Add words or phrases to connect related ideas that lack transitions.
4. Does the concluding section restate the main idea? Does it give the audience something to think about?	Place a checkmark above the restatement of the main idea in the concluding section and underline the insight offered to readers.	Add a statement about your key points or a final observation about the importance of your ideas.

Revision Checklist: Peer Review

Exchange your essay with a classmate, or read it aloud to your partner. As you read and comment on your classmate's essay, focus on the organization and on how clearly the two folk tales have been compared and contrasted. Help each other identify parts of the draft that need strengthening, reworking, or even a new approach.

What To Look For	Notes for My Partner
1. Does the introduction grab the audience's attention and state your main idea?	
2. Does the essay include examples of ways in which the folk tales are alike and ways in which they are different? Is each key point of comparison supported by well-chosen and sufficient textual evidence, including facts and concrete details?	
3. Are appropriate and varied transitions used to connect, compare, and contrast ideas?	
4. Does the concluding section restate the main idea? Does it give the reader something to think about?	

Edit

Edit your essay to correct spelling, grammar, and punctuation errors.

How can the theme of a story convey a viewpoint about life?

You will read:

▶ **AN INFORMATIONAL TEXT**
How Authors Convey the Theme

▶ **A SHORT STORY**
"The White Umbrella"

You will write:

▶ **A LITERARY ANALYSIS**
How does the author of "The White Umbrella" convey the theme of the story?

How Authors Convey the Theme

by Martin Rashad

NOTES

Simply put, the theme of a work of literature conveys a larger message or lesson about life or human nature. The theme of a story is different from the topic. The topic of a story, poem, or another work of literature is the subject that the author chooses to write about. A topic can be: a person, an idea, an event, or an emotion. The theme relates to the topic, but it differs from it in that it expresses a message, lesson, or central idea about the topic.

For example, suppose that the topic of a story is
10 friendship—perhaps the friendship between two sixth-grade students of different cultures. Although the topic of the story is the friendship between these two students, the theme of the story may be that the power of friendship can overcome differences. Therefore, although the theme relates to the subject, it expresses a message or lesson about friendship. However, keep in mind that a writer will not come right out and say "This story's theme is that friendship can overcome differences." Instead it is up to the reader to discover the theme.

How do authors convey the theme of a work? The first
20 thing to consider is the title. The title may hint at the theme by highlighting an important idea, setting, image, or character.

Plot is the action of a story. It is another way in which authors convey the theme. For example, the main character may take actions to overcome a problem or conflict. The way the main character resolves the conflict may give you important clues to the theme.

You may also determine the theme by closely examining the main character. What does the main character say? What do other characters say about this character? What is striking
30 about the character's thoughts and actions? As you read, ask yourself what lesson the main character learns over the course of the story. You will likely find the theme if you determine the lesson.

Other literary elements, including setting, images, and stylistic elements, can also hint at the theme. Also, note when authors create a particularly striking image or emphasize a thought or idea by repeating it. These may be included to convey the theme of the story.

Discuss and Decide

Reread lines 19–38. With a partner, discuss ways that authors develop the theme. Decide how the title, plot, characters, and other literary elements might convey the theme to the reader.

The White Umbrella

by Gish Jen

When I was twelve, my mother went to work without telling me or my little sister.

"Not that we need the second income." The lilt of her accent drifted from the kitchen up to the top of the stairs, where Mona and I were listening.

"No," said my father, in a barely audible voice. "Not like the Lee family."

The Lees were the only other Chinese family in town. I remembered how sorry my parents had felt for Mrs. Lee when 10 she started waitressing downtown the year before; and so when my mother began coming home late, I didn't say anything, and tried to keep Mona from saying anything either.

"But why shouldn't I?" she argued. "Lots of people's mothers work."

"Those are American people," I said.

"So what do you think we are? I can do the pledge of allegiance with my eyes closed."

Nevertheless, she tried to be discreet; and if my mother wasn't home by 5:30, we would start cooking by ourselves, to 20 make sure dinner would be on time. Mona would wash the vegetables and put on the rice; I would chop.

For weeks we wondered what kind of work she was doing. I imagined that she was selling perfume, testing dessert recipes for the local newspaper. Or maybe she was working for the florist. Now that she had learned to drive, she might be delivering boxes of roses to people.

"I don't think so," said Mona as we walked to our piano lesson after school. "She would've hit something by now."

A gust of wind littered the street with leaves.

30 "Maybe we better hurry up," she went on, looking at the sky. "It's going to pour."

"But we're too early." Her lesson didn't begin until 4:00, mine until 4:30, so we usually tried to walk as slowly as we could. "And anyway, those aren't the kind of clouds that rain. Those are cumulus clouds."

We arrived out of breath and wet.

"Oh, you poor, poor dears," said old Miss Crosman. "Why don't you call me the next time it's like this out? If your mother won't drive you, I can come pick you up."

40 "No, that's okay," I answered. Mona wrung her hair out on Miss Crosman's rug. "We just couldn't get the roof of our car to close, is all. We took it to the beach last summer and got sand in the mechanism." I pronounced this last word carefully, as if the credibility of my lie depended on its middle syllable. "It's never been the same." I thought for a second. "It's a convertible."

"Well then make yourselves at home." She exchanged looks with Eugenie Roberts, whose lesson we were interrupting. Eugenie smiled good-naturedly. "The towels are in the closet across from the bathroom."

50 Huddling at the end of Miss Crosman's nine-foot leatherette couch, Mona and I watched Eugenie play. She was a grade ahead of me and, according to school rumor, had a boyfriend in high school. I believed it. . . . She had auburn hair, blue eyes, and, I noted with a particular pang, a pure white folding umbrella.

Dicuss and Decide

Reread lines 18–45. With a small group, discuss why the narrator lies to Miss Crosman. Cite specific evidence from the text.

"I can't see," whispered Mona.

"So clean your glasses."

"My glasses *are* clean. You're in the way."

I looked at her. "They look dirty to me."

60 "That's because *your* glasses are dirty."

Eugenie came bouncing to the end of her piece.

"Oh! Just stupendous!" Miss Crosman hugged her, then looked up as Eugenie's mother walked in. "Stupendous!" she said again. "Oh! Mrs. Roberts! Your daughter has a gift, a real gift. It's an honor to teach her."

Mrs. Roberts, radiant with pride, swept her daughter out of the room as if she were royalty, born to the piano bench. Watching the way Eugenie carried herself, I sat up, and concentrated so hard on sucking in my stomach that I did not

70 realize until the Robertses were gone that Eugenie had left her umbrella. As Mona began to play, I jumped and ran to the window, meaning to call to them—only to see their brake lights flash then fade at the stop sign at the comer. As if to allow them passage, the rain had let up; a quivering sun lit their way.

The umbrella glowed like a scepter on the blue carpet while Mona, slumping over the keyboard, managed to eke out a fair rendition of a catfight. At the end of the piece, Miss Crosman asked her to stand up.

"Stay right there," she said, then came back a minute

80 later with a towel to cover the bench. "You must be cold," she continued. "Shall I call your mother and have her bring over some dry clothes?"

"No," answered Mona. "She won't come because she . . . "

"She's too busy," I broke in from the back of the room.

"I see." Miss Crosman sighed and shook her head a little. "Your glasses are filthy, honey," she said to Mona. "Shall I clean them for you?"

Sisterly embarrassment seized me. Why hadn't Mona wiped her lenses when I told her to? As she resumed abuse of the piano, I stared at the umbrella. I wanted to open it, twirl it around by its slender silver handle; I wanted to dangle it from my wrist on the way to school the way the other girls did. I wondered what Miss Crosman would say if I offered to bring it to Eugenie at school tomorrow. She would be impressed with my consideration for others; Eugenie would be pleased to have it back; and I would have possession of the umbrella for an entire night. I looked at it again, toying with the idea of asking for one for Christmas. I knew, however, how my mother would react.

"Things," she would say. "What's the matter with a raincoat? All you want is things, just like an American."

✳

Sitting down for my lesson, I was careful to keep the towel under me and sit up straight.

"I'll bet you can't see a thing either," said Miss Crosman, reaching for my glasses. "And you can relax, you poor dear. . . . This isn't a boot camp."

When Miss Crosman finally allowed me to start playing I played extra well, as well as I possibly could. See, I told her with my fingers. You don't have to feel sorry for me.

"That was wonderful," said Miss Crosman. "Oh! Just wonderful."

An entire constellation rose in my heart.

"And guess what," I announced proudly. "I have a surprise for you."

Then I played a second piece for her, a much more difficult one that she had not assigned.

Discuss and Decide

Reread lines 62–111. With a partner, discuss your impression of Miss Crosman. Explain your impression by citing specific evidence from the text.

© Houghton Mifflin Harcourt Publishing Company

"Oh! That was stupendous," she said without hugging me. "Stupendous! You are a genius, young lady. If your mother had started you younger, you'd be playing like Eugenie Roberts by now!"

120

I looked at the keyboard, wishing that I had still a third, even more difficult piece to play for her. I wanted to tell her that I was the school spelling bee champion, that I wasn't ticklish, that I could do karate.

"My mother is a concert pianist," I said.

She looked at me for a long moment, then finally, without saying anything, hugged me. I didn't say anything about bringing the umbrella to Eugenie at school.

The steps were dry when Mona and I sat down to wait for my

130 mother.

"Do you want to wait inside?" Miss Crosman looked anxiously at the sky.

"No," I said. "Our mother will be here any minute."

"In a while," said Mona.

"Any minute," I said again, even though my mother had been at least twenty minutes late every week since she started working.

According to the church clock across the street we had been waiting twenty-five minutes when Miss Crosman came out

140 again.

"Shall I give you ladies a ride home?"

"No," I said. "Our mother is coming any minute."

"Shall I at least give her a call and remind her you're here? Maybe she forgot about you."

Dicuss and Decide

Reread lines 113–120. With a partner, discuss why the narrator has learned to play a second, more difficult, piece? Cite specific evidence from the text in your discussion.

1. Analyze | 2. Practice | 3. Perform

"I don't think she *forgot*," said Mona.

"Shall I give her a call anyway? Just to be safe?"

"I bet she already left," I said. "How could she forget about us?"

Miss Crosman went in to call.

150   "There's no answer," she said, coming back out.

"See, she's on her way," I said.

"Are you sure you wouldn't like to come in?"

"No," said Mona.

"Yes," I said. I pointed at my sister. "She meant yes too. She meant no, she wouldn't like to go in."

Miss Crosman looked at her watch. "It's 5:30 now, ladies. My pot roast will be coming out in fifteen minutes. Maybe you'd like to come in and have some then?"

"My mother's almost here," I said. "She's on her way."

160   We watched and watched the street. I tried to imagine what my mother was doing; I tried to imagine her writing messages in the sky, even though I knew she was afraid of planes. I watched as the branches of Miss Crosman's big willow tree started to sway; they had all been trimmed to exactly the same height off the ground, so that they looked beautiful, like hair in the wind.

It started to rain.

"Miss Crosman is coming out again," said Mona.

"Don't let her talk you into going inside," I whispered.

170   "Why not?"

"Because that would mean that Mom isn't really coming any minute."

"But she isn't," said Mona. "She's *working.*"

"Shhh! Miss Crosman is going to hear you."

My mother began to back up, but the car behind us honked. Luckily, the light turned green right after that. She sighed in relief.

300   "What were you saying, Mona?" she asked.

We wouldn't have hit the car behind us that hard if he hadn't been moving too, but as it was our car bucked violently, throwing us all first back and then forward.

"Uh oh," said Mona when we stopped. "*Another* accident."

I was relieved to have attention diverted from the umbrella. Then I noticed my mother's head, tilted back onto the seat. Her eyes were closed.

"Mom!" I screamed. "Mom! Wake up!"

She opened her eyes. "Please don't yell," she said. "Enough
310   people are going to yell already."

"I thought you were dead," I said, starting to cry. "I thought you were dead."

She turned around, looked at me intently, then put her hand to my forehead.

"Sick," she confirmed. "Some kind of sick is giving you crazy ideas."

As the man from the car behind us started tapping on the window, I moved the umbrella away from my leg. Then Mona and my mother were getting out of the car. I got out after
320   them; and while everyone else was inspecting the damage we'd done, I threw the umbrella down a sewer.

Close Read

As you reread the last paragraph of the story, underline what the narrator does with the umbrella. What larger lesson about life or human nature might the narrator have learned? What does this action suggest about the theme of the story?

_____

_____

Respond to Questions on Step 3 Sources

Use your notes and refer to the short story as you answer the questions. Your answers to will help you write your essay.

1 What does the word *stupendous* mean in these lines from "The White Umbrella"?

> "'Stupendous!' she said again. 'Oh! Mrs. Roberts! Your daughter has a gift, a real gift. It's an honor to teach her.'" (lines 63–65)

    a. tragic   **b.** wonderful

    c. adorable   **d.** beautiful

2 Which word from the lines of text in Question 1 best helps you understand the meaning of *stupendous*?

    a. teach   **b.** again

    c. gift   **d.** Oh!

3 What does the word *radiant* mean in these lines from "The White Umbrella"?

> "Mrs. Roberts, radiant with pride, swept her daughter out of the room as if she were royalty, born to the piano bench." (lines 66–67)

    a. beaming   **b.** light-hearted

    c. gorgeous   **d.** confident

4 Which word from the lines of text in Question 3 best helps you understand the meaning of *radiant*?

    a. swept   **b.** piano

    c. royalty   **d.** pride

5 **Prose Constructed-Response** Why does the narrator repeatedly lie about the fact that her mother is working? How do her lies reveal her feelings? Cite specific evidence from the text.

_____

_____

_____

_____

6 **Prose Constructed-Response** The author emphasizes the image of the white umbrella throughout the story. What does the white umbrella stand for? What does it hint about the theme?

_____

_____

_____

_____

7 **Prose Constructed-Response** How does the accident at the end of the story relate to the narrator's feelings about her mother? How does it relate to the theme?

_____

_____

_____

_____

1. Analyze   2. Practice   3. Perform

Part 2: Write

Write a literary analysis that answers the question: How does the author of "The White Umbrella" convey the theme of the story?

Plan

Use the graphic organizer to help you outline the structure of your literary analysis.

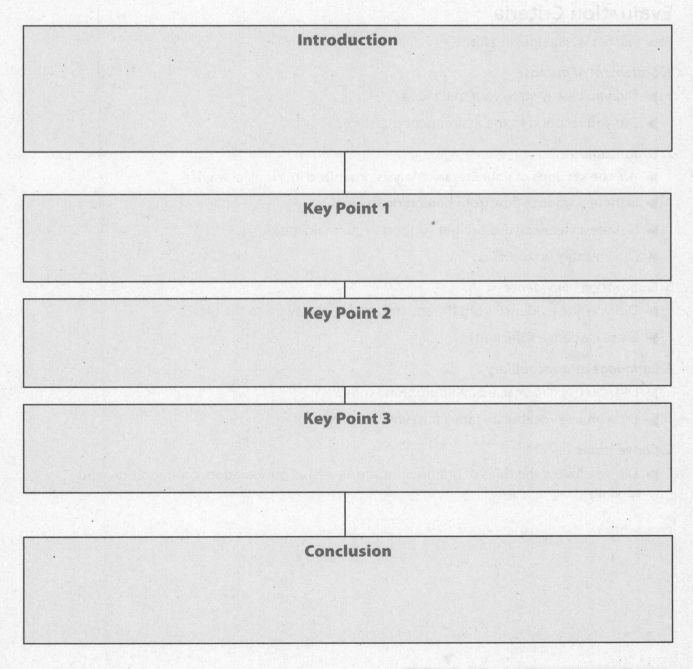

Introduction

Key Point 1

Key Point 2

Key Point 3

Conclusion

Draft

 Use your notes and completed graphic organizer to write a first draft of your literary analysis.

Revise and Edit

 Look back over your essay and compare it to the Evaluation Criteria. Revise your literary analysis and edit it to correct spelling, grammar, and punctuation errors.

Evaluation Criteria

Your teacher will be looking for:

1. *Statement of purpose*

▶ Did you clearly state your main idea?

▶ Did you respond to the assignment question?

2. *Organization*

▶ Are the sections of your literary analysis organized in a logical way?

▶ Is there a smooth flow from beginning to end?

▶ Is there a clear conclusion that supports your main idea?

▶ Did you stay on topic?

3. *Elaboration of evidence*

▶ Did you cite evidence from the sources, and is it relevant to the topic?

▶ Is the evidence sufficient?

4. *Language and vocabulary*

▶ Did you use a formal, essay-appropriate tone?

▶ Did you use vocabulary familiar to your audience?

5. *Conventions*

▶ Did you follow the rules of grammar usage as well as punctuation, capitalization, and spelling?

On Your Own

RESEARCH SIMULATION

Argumentative Essay

Your school is participating in a citywide essay contest about bullying. The goal of the contest is to raise awareness of the impact bullying has on young people and to propose ways to discourage this type of behavior in your community.

First you will review two articles on bullying. After you have reviewed these sources, you will answer some questions about them. You should first skim the sources and the questions and then go back and read them carefully.

In Part 2, you will write an argumentative essay about whether you agree or disagree that parents should be held accountable if their children engage in bullying.

Time Management: Argumentative Task

There are two parts to most formal writing tests. Both parts of the tests are timed, so it's important to use your limited time wisely.

Part 1: Read Sources and Answer Questions

Preview the Assignment

35 minutes

You will have 35 minutes to read two sources and decide whether you agree or disagree that parents should be held accountable if their children are bullies. You will also answer questions that will help you plan your essay on the topic.

35 minutes! That's not much time.

Preview the questions. This will help you know which information you'll need to find as you read.

How Many?

How many pages of reading?

→ How many multiple-choice questions?

→ How many prose constructed-response questions?

How do you plan to use the 35 minutes?

Underline, circle, and take notes as you read. You probably won't have time to reread.

Estimated time to read:

This is a lot to do in a short time.

    Source #1: "White House Conference Tackles Bullying" — ____ minutes

    Source #2: "Parenting a Bully: What Are the Responsibilities?" — ____ minutes

Estimated time to answer questions? — ____ minutes

Total   **35**   **minutes**

Any concerns?

_____

_____

Part 2: Write the Essay

70

How much time do you have? Pay attention to the clock!

Plan and Write an Argumentative Essay

70 minutes

You will have 70 minutes to plan, write, revise, and edit your essay.

Your Plan

Before you start to write, decide on your precise claim and reasons. Then think about the evidence you will use to support your reasons.

How do you plan to use the 70 minutes?

Be sure to leave enough time for this step.

Estimated time for planning the essay?		minutes
Estimated time for writing?		minutes
Estimated time for editing?		minutes
Estimated time for checking spelling, grammar, and punctuation?		minutes
Total	**70**	**minutes**

Notes:

_____

_____

_____

_____

Reread your essay, making sure that the points are clear. Check that there are no spelling or punctuation mistakes.

▶ Your Task

> Your principal has asked students to participate in a citywide essay contest about bullying. The contest rules require you to take a position on whether or not parents should be held accountable if their children engage in bullying. In researching the topic, you have identified two sources you will use in planning your argumentative essay.

After you have reviewed the sources, you will answer some questions about them. Briefly skim the sources and the three questions that follow. Then, go back and read the sources carefully so you will have the information you will need to answer the questions. Take notes on the sources as you read. You may refer back to your notes at any time during Part 1 or Part 2 of the performance task.

▶ Part 1 (35 minutes)

You will now read the sources. After carefully reading the sources, use the rest of the time in Part 1 to answer the three questions about them. Though your answers to these questions will help you think about what you have read and plan your essay, they will also be scored as part of the test.

SOURCE #1:
White House Conference Tackles *Bullying*

by Mimi Hall, USA TODAY

WASHINGTON — President Obama, a father of pre-teens, convenes a day-long White House Conference on Preventing Bullying today.

It marks the first time a president has brought so much attention to the difficult and sometimes devastating problem.

The goal of the conference, according to the White House, is to dispel a commonly held belief that bullying is a normal rite of passage for kids and share ideas about how the federal government and communities can help prevent bullying and

10 deal with its consequences.

"This isn't an issue that makes headlines every day, but it is an issue that affects every single young person in the country," Obama says in a video about the conference posted Wednesday on Facebook.

First lady Michelle Obama, appearing with him, says the issue is "something we care about not only as president and first lady but also as parents. It's tough enough being a kid today, and our children deserve the chance to learn and grow without constantly being picked on, made fun of—or worse."

20 Government statistics show that roughly one in three middle and high school students report being bullied. Research shows that bullying adversely affects children's mental health, academic success and ability to relate to other kids, says Mary Wakefield, who runs the Health Resources and Services Administration at the Department of Health and Human Services. It also has "lasting emotional consequences."

Eight hours after Obama's video was posted Wednesday, more than 2,300 people had clicked "like," far more than on any recent White House post.

30 "This is an issue that resonates with all of us," says Melody Barnes, director of Obama's Domestic Policy Council.

Smalley[1] says he has been working with students at three local high schools through a program called Stand for the Silent. Together, they spread the message that everyone plays a role in bullying—the bullies, the bullied and the many bystanders who don't stop it.

He and the high school students he works with are typically swarmed after their presentation. "Kids hug us and cry," Smalley says. "Even the bullies. They want to do something

40 about it."

He says the federal government can help such local efforts by providing guidelines to schools.

"Right now, most schools don't know what to do in a bullying case," Smalley says.

The White House conference is part of the administration's recent efforts to address the issue. Obama and his aides already have:

- Hosted the Department of Education's first "summit" on bullying in August 2010. "The problem of bullying has been

50 shrouded in myth and misunderstanding for far too many years," Education Secretary Arne Duncan said then. "We simply have not taken the problem of bullying seriously enough."

He said high-level attention to the issue is needed because bullying is a school safety issue.

"It is troubling in and of itself, but bullying is doubly dangerous because if left unattended, it can rapidly escalate

---

[1] **Kirk Smalley** a construction worker from Perkins, OK, and his family have suffered the effects of bullying firsthand.

into even more serious violence and abuse," Duncan said.

- Operated a website, stopbullying.gov, to provide information
60 to kids, parents, teachers, schools, churches, community
    groups and state governments.

- Informed school districts that some cases of bullying can be
  prosecuted under federal anti-discrimination laws.

- Taped public service announcements for the It Gets Better
  campaign aimed at stopping bullying of gay and lesbian
  students.

Am I on Track?

Actual Time Spent Reading

Parenting a Bully:

What Are the Responsibilities?

by Damien Steiner

NOTES

Parents may not realize that their child is a bully. It can be a difficult truth to learn no matter who delivers the news, be it a teacher, a friend, a family member, or a bullied child's parent. The bully's parents may protest and may be unable at first to acknowledge the truth.

Once parents have accepted the problem, there are ways to work with their child. It can be helpful to have a school counselor or mental health professional provide suggestions for how to deal with the situation, which may include having
10   a direct conversation with their child. Bullies usually have a reason for their behavior. They may have seen another person act like a bully to get something she wanted, they may be feeling insecure and bullying is a way for them to ask for help, or they may have been bullied themselves and are acting out in response. Parents should have an open dialogue with their child and create an environment in which the child feels he can share what he is feeling without judgment.

Even if the bullying does not stem from any one source, there are steps that can be taken to help the child. Both parents
20   and school officials can monitor the child to prevent further bullying. Parents can withdraw certain privileges when they learn of bullying behavior, but replace these privileges with positive activities, such as limiting time online in order to help an elderly neighbor. Developing strategies for dealing with angry feelings is another way to avoid bullying behavior in future.

Bullies can begin to make amends by apologizing to those they have bullied or by doing something helpful for them. Parents can act as positive role models for their child. Being

30 a role model provides the child with someone to look up to. Teaching leadership skills is another way to direct energy in a positive way.

As of October 2010, 47 states in the U.S. had anti-bullying laws. These anti-bullying laws are seen as a preventative measure, but the specifics of these laws vary from state to state. Anti-bullying laws apply to both bullying in person, as well as cyberbullying, which is bullying on the computer or over the phone. If an act of bullying is committed over the phone or on the computer, parents can be held legally responsible for their child's

40 actions.

Anti-bullying laws can require parents of minors who are bullies to pay juvenile court fees or monetary damages in civil suits for emotional distress to the victim. However, sometimes these laws may land them in jail. In California, parents can be imprisoned for failure to exercise appropriate supervision over their children.

Am I on Track?

Actual Time Spent Reading

Part 1 Questions

Answer the following questions. You may refer to your reading notes, and you should cite text evidence in your responses. Your answers to these questions will be scored. You will be able to refer to your answers as you write your essay in Part 2.

1 Using context clues, what is a synonym for the word "acknowledge" in the following sentence in Source #2? "The bully's parents may protest and may be unable at first to acknowledge the truth."

   a. argue

   b. understand

   c. admit

   d. deny

2 **Prose Constructed-Response** Based on the information in Source #1, why did the president and his administration feel that a day-long conference was needed? What was the primary goal of the White House conference? Provide evidence for each piece of information from the source.

_____

_____

_____

_____

_____

3 **Prose Constructed-Response** Based on the information in Source #2, briefly summarize the advice given to parents of a bully. Be sure to avoid plagiarism in your summary.

_____

_____

_____

_____

_____

You now have 70 minutes to review your notes and sources and to plan, draft, revise, and edit your essay. While you may use your notes and refer to the sources, your essay must represent your own original work. You may refer to your responses to Part 1 questions, but you cannot change those answers. Now read your assignment and the information about how your writing will be scored; then begin your work.

Your Assignment

The deadline for the citywide essay contest is approaching. It is time to start writing your argumentative essay. Remember, your essay should explain whether you agree or disagree with the idea that parents should be held responsible for their child's bullying. When writing your essay, find ways to use information from the two sources to support your argument. A good argumentative essay should include a strong claim, and it should address opposing arguments.

Argumentative Essay Scoring

Your essay will be scored using the following:

1. **Organization/purpose:** How well did you express your claim, address opposing claims, and support your claim with logical ideas? How well did your ideas flow from beginning to end? How effective was your introduction and conclusion?

2. **Evidence/elaboration:** How well did you incorporate relevant information from the sources? Did you use specific titles or numbers in referring to the sources? How strong is the elaboration for your ideas? Did you clearly state your ideas in your own words in a way that is appropriate for your audience and purpose?

3. **Conventions:** How well did you follow the rules of grammar, punctuation, capitalization, and spelling?

Now begin work on your essay. Manage your time carefully so that you can:

- plan your essay, using your notes
- write your essay
- revise and edit your final draft

TASK 2

© Houghton Mifflin Harcourt Publishing Company

RESEARCH SIMULATION

Informative Essay

You are writing an article for your school newspaper about a bike path planned for your town. The teacher who supervises the paper has asked you to focus on what features of a bike path are most important.

You will begin your task by reviewing three source articles. After you have reviewed these sources, you will answer questions about them. You should first skim the sources and the questions; then you should go back and read the sources carefully.

In Part 2, you will write an informative essay in the form of a newspaper article about the criteria people use to judge a good biking trail.

Time Management: Informative Task

There are two parts to most formal writing tests. Both parts of the tests are timed, so it's important to use your limited time wisely.

Part 1: Read Sources and Answer Questions

Preview the Assignment

35 minutes

You will have 35 minutes to read three sources that will help you decide which criteria should be used to choose a bike trail. You will also answer questions that will help you plan an informative essay.

35 minutes! That's not much time.

How Many?

Preview the questions. This will help you know which information you'll need to find as you read.

How many pages of reading?

How many multiple-choice questions?

How many prose constructed-response questions?

How do you plan to use the 35 minutes?

Underline, circle, and take notes as you read. You probably won't have time to reread.

This is a lot to do in a short time.

Estimated time to read:

Source #1: "Best American Bike Trails" _____ minutes

Source #2: "Top Five Places to Mountain Bike" _____ minutes

Source #3: "Not Your Typical Mountain Biking Trail" _____ minutes

Estimated time to answer questions? _____ minutes

Total   **35   minutes**

Any concerns?

_____

_____

Part 2: Write the Essay

How much time do you have? Pay attention to the clock!

Plan and Write an Informative Essay

→ **70 minutes**

You will have 70 minutes to plan, write, revise, and edit your essay.

Your Plan

Before you start to write, decide on your precise claim and reasons. Then think about the evidence you will use to support your reasons.

How do you plan to use the 70 minutes?

Estimated time for planning the essay?		minutes
Estimated time for writing?		minutes
Estimated time for editing?		minutes
Estimated time for checking spelling, grammar, and punctuation?		minutes
Total	**70**	**minutes**

Be sure to leave enough time for this step.

Notes:

_____

_____

_____

_____

Reread your essay, making sure that the points are clear. Check that there are no spelling or punctuation mistakes.

▶ Your Task

> You are writing an article for your school newspaper about a bike path planned for your town. The focus of your article will be the features that good bike paths or trails should have. To begin the assignment, you will review three sources about bike trails.

After reviewing the three sources, you must answer some questions about them. You should first skim the sources and questions. Then go back and read them carefully.

▶ Part 1 (35 minutes)

After carefully reading the sources, use the rest of the time in Part 1 to answer the three questions about them. Though your answers to these questions will help you think about what you have read and plan your essay, they will also be scored as part of the test.

SOURCE #1:
Best American Bike Trails
Forbes Traveler

by Jeff Wallach, ForbesTraveler.com

Bicycling has come a long way since you pedaled the old neighborhood on your Sting Ray with the sissy bar and purple banana seat. Just as you eventually graduated to a ten-speed, road bikes have evolved significantly, and then there's the highly popular category of mountain biking, which combines the pleasures (and pain) of road trips with the yee-haw attitude of wilderness adventure. Whether you choose a mountain bike or a road bike, isn't it time for you to venture outside of the neighborhood and take on some of the terrific bike trails
10 scattered across the nation?

From dirt tracks to converted railroad tracks, great trails throughout the U.S. provide a variety of terrain, scenery, amenities, challenge, and overall experience for riders of differing abilities and intentions. We've rounded up ten of the best for your leg-pumping pleasure.

For many riders, surface is a key ingredient of a great trail. These cyclists want to pedal happily and enjoy the scenery without looking at the ground to avoid bumps, roots, potholes, and other potential hazards. Sixty-eight-year-old Polly
20 Mayberry, of Winston-Salem, N.C., is such a rider. Mayberry and her husband pedal about 1,000 miles annually, and provide descriptions, logistical information, and links to additions sources about their favorite trails on their website, great-trails.com. Mayberry chooses Missouri's Katy Trail as one of the nation's best, in part because of its great surface. "As older riders, surface matters to us," Mayberry says. "We don't want to ride a trail that's too rough. The Katy Trail would be a ten because of the beauty of the territory and the trail surface—mostly of hard-packed limestone. It's basically flat and it's an
30 easy ride for people of all ages. You can ride for mile after mile seeing nothing but country."

For cyclists, great scenery is another important component of the best trails—you might as well be chugging past beautiful and interesting sights. Mayberry ranks the Hiawatha Trail in Montana and Idaho highly, largely for the views rolling past. It's also one of many former railroad lines that has been converted to a bike trail. "This is probably the most scenic bike trail in the country," she reports. "It's up on a mountain and hard to find." The route features ten tunnels, including the 1.66-mile Taft

40 Tunnel, which takes riders beneath the Idaho-Montana state line. The 15-mile jaunt also includes crossings of seven trestles. "The trestles are extremely high and offer fantastic views of beautiful, rugged mountains," Mayberry says. "Children love the trail because of the tunnels. And there are waterfalls."

Joe "Metal Cowboy" Kurmaskie likes scenery as much as anyone, but he believes the very best bike trails need to have something more than just great views. A performer, bike advocate, and author of three best-selling books about bicycle travel (most recently *Momentum is Your Friend*), Kurmaskie

50 has logged more than 127,000 miles on wheels. One of his favorite routes is along the Underground Railroad Trail, stretching from Alabama to Ohio and beyond into Canada.

Kurmaskie says, "A great trail doesn't have to have *National Geographic*-quality scenery, but it needs something visually, culturally, or historically unique—like a trail linking great barbecue pits in the South, or one that follows a route to ten famed baseball stadiums, or that takes you past the world's largest ball of string. Every good trail simply needs to be unique and have a theme, even if you make up the theme yourself."

60 He adds that a high point of this historic ride is that "all the towns along it are hip to bikers—there are no *Cool Hand Luke* moments anymore. People are ready and waiting for bikers."

As Kurmaskie notes, the Underground Railroad Trail "highlights the best hospitality of small towns with quite a bit of our country's history woven into the ride." Hospitality and service are hallmarks of great rides—many cyclists want to sprint or glide toward a finish line with a special café or brewpub waiting. On longer rides, especially, the quality of

services can help turn a slog into a comfortable journey broken
70 up by hot baths at quaint inns, a memorable breakfast, or even a
place to restock on everything from food to excitement.

Jim Sayer is the Executive Director of the non-profit
Adventure Cycling Association, which publishes a magazine,
maps, and other resources for bikers, offers tours and classes,
and works to inspire people of all ages to travel by bicycle.
Sayer agrees that safety and comfort are major components
of the best trails. "Traffic volume, facilities, and how the
trails themselves are designed and maintained all matter," he
says. "Great trails should go through communities and towns
80 with shops and campgrounds and other amenities." That's
one reason why he chooses The Transamerica Trail, running
between Virginia and Oregon, as one of the nation's best. "No
other bike trail does a better job taking you through America's
heartland and its small towns, and no other trail compares for
capturing America in all its variety and heritage. Finishing
this trail leaves people feeling like this is one of the greatest
countries in the world for its people and landscape."

But some riders won't be happy spinning through quaint
towns and sipping iced lattes—they want to hurl themselves
90 at challenging terrain. For these hard-core riders seeking a
more adventurous experience, Sayer recommends the Great
Divide Trail, which follows the route of the Continental Divide
through some of the most mountainous regions of North
America. "It's the longest mountain bike ride anywhere in the
world and gives a sense of remoteness that's unusual in the U.S.
these days," Sayer reports. "Other trails share space with hikers
and horseback riders. This is the longest trail a bicyclist can
take to feel remote and out there and away from civilization."

Many cyclists choose a single section of a trail to ride,
100 whether for a few hours or for many days, or return to ride
new sections of the same trails for years until they complete
an entire route. And with trails like the Transamerica, which
stretches more than 4,000 miles, or the Great Divide Mountain
Bike Trail, that huffs over 200,000 feet of elevation gain, that's a
good idea for most free-wheeling travelers.

Am I on Track?

Actual Time Spent Reading

Top Five Places to Mountain Bike

Coast to Coast Mountain Bike Meccas

by Beth Puliti, About.com Guide

NOTES

Let's face it: We'd all like to spend days on end exploring every last spot of sweet singletrack[1] this country has to offer. But we can't. (I know, the truth hurts.) So, after riding and researching some of the very best mountain bike destinations in the U.S., I've narrowed it down to five must-see spots. Start with this list the next time you're searching for a prime place to pedal.

1. Moab, Utah There's a reason everyone talks about Moab. Touted as having "the greatest mountain biking on the planet,"
10 Moab's variety of trails and terrain means mountain bikers of all levels will have a fantastic time.

Perhaps the most popular mountain bike trail in the world, Moab's Slickrock trail welcomes more than 100,000 visitors per year. But it's not the only trail in town. Countless more, including Sovereign and Amasa Back, offer moderately technical options. Klondike Bluffs and the Intrepid Trail System among others offer a technically-easy ride.

No matter what trail you choose, you'll be riding in the desert. So, plan accordingly.

20 **2. Fruita, Colorado** Located in western Colorado's high desert, Fruita offers hundreds of miles of trails that will please just about anyone looking for a thrill.

Ride the Book Cliffs area for wide-open views of the Grand Valley basin. Got some endurance? Chutes and Ladders, the classic run, offers steep climbs and descents that aren't for the

---

[1] **singletrack:** is a term used to describe a trail that is only wide enough for one person or mountain biker at a time. Singletrack is the most popular or sought after type of mountain bike trail.

weak. At 2,000 vertical feet above the basin, The Edge Loop—a designated International Mountain Bicycling Association Epic trail—offers tight singletrack.

30 Rockier and a bit more technical than trails at Book Cliffs, the Kokopelli Trails are geared toward intermediate to expert mountain bikers. Those looking for smaller scale riding can survey the natural beauty of Fruita's landscape while taking a spin on the 18 Road Trails.

3. Asheville, North Carolina Nestled between the Blue Ridge and Appalachian mountains, the energetic town of Asheville offers as much excitement as its natural surroundings. But make no mistake, the real attractions lie outside downtown, within the western North Carolina mountains.

Look no further than the Pisgah Mountains for supreme
40 mountain biking. Here, singletrack weaves past waterfalls and opens up to meadows.

Just a short distance southeast, more trails—hundreds of miles of them, actually—exist in DuPont State Forest. Unlike Pisgah's red-clay, DuPont's trails are a mix of grippy granite and sandy soil. Take a trip to see for yourself why Asheville has been nicknamed the Moab of the South!

4. East Burke, Vermont East Burke may seem like it's in the middle of nowhere, but Vermont's Northeast Kingdom is just a couple hours from the cities of Burlington and
50 Montreal—and you better believe it's worth the drive. The tiny town was put on the map in part by Kingdom Trails, a mountain bike mecca that offers more than 100 miles of non-motorized trails.

It's not hard to see why the International Mountain Bicycling Association designated Kingdom Trails an "Epic" ride. The place is brimming with flowing singletrack, well-manicured terrain and beautiful landscape. Trails are easily identifiable with beginner, intermediate and advanced markings. Belted cows, maple syrup tubing and sugar shacks dot the landscape
60 for a truly New England experience.

© Houghton Mifflin Harcourt Publishing Company

5. Park City, Utah Located in the Western edge of the Rocky Mountains, Park City offers some of the most breathtaking scenery around—literally. At 8,000 feet above sea level, the 20-or-so-mile Mid Mountain Trail boasts close to 3,000 feet of up-and-down altitude change. Give yourself ample time to acclimate.

The recommended Mid Mountain route starts at Silver Lake at Deer Valley Resort, but you can create your own ride by taking Sweeney North, Sweeney South, Daly Canyon or Deer Valley
70 to Mid Mountain. No matter which route you take, prepare to climb!

Sure, some trails are mighty rocky and, yes, there are a few unrelenting uphills, but Park City offers a variety of trails, fit for both beginner and experienced mountain bikers. Map your route accordingly.

Am I on Track?

Actual Time Spent Reading

Not Your Typical Mountain Biking Trail

from *American Bikers Association Magazine*

by Aaron Dunphy

Maybe you love off-road cycling, and maybe you've done some bicycle training in your time. But even if you've ridden on some amazing trails, you might not have imagined cycling like this.

Indoor Cycling

Gone are the days when you need an outdoor trail to go mountain biking. Seven months out of the year, indoor parks allow bikers to ride straight through the off season—regardless of waning daylight, freezing temperatures, and the dangerous snow, slush, and ice conditions outside. At Ray's Indoor Mountain Bike Park, located in Milwaukee, Wisconsin, riders
10 balance on beams, pedal through rock gardens, and practice their 360-degree flips into cushioned foam pits—landings that would be dangerous to attempt on a dirt trail.

Slickrock Riding

Perhaps the most well-known slickrock bike trek is Slickrock Trail in Moab, Utah. Here, the terrain is made up of huge rocks, making the environs look like the surface of the moon. As a result, the trail is impossibly steep, but, unlike on the moon, gravity asserts itself here with tremendous force. The saving grace on an otherwise harrowing trek is the unique sandstone riding surface. The trail acts like sandpaper, giving
20 the cyclist grippy traction on all but the steepest twists and turns.

NOTES

Blue Ribbon Cycling

The section of the Tahoe Rim Trail between Tahoe Meadows and Spooner Summit has an epic view of the largest alpine lake in North America. So epic in fact, that the International Mountain Bicycling Association bestowed this particular 21.8-mile stretch with its Epics award. The whole trail passes through two states (California and Nevada), six counties, one state park (Lake Tahoe–Nevada State Park), and three National Forests (the Tahoe, Toiyabe, and Eldorado 30 National Forests). With all the mind-boggling views of Lake Tahoe, don't forget to keep your eyes on the trail.

Am I on Track?

Actual Time Spent Reading

Part 1 Questions

Answer the following questions. You may refer to your reading notes, and you should cite text evidence in your responses. Your answers to these questions will be scored. You will be able to refer to your answers as you write your essay in Part 2.

1 **Prose Constructed-Response** What are the most important requirements, or criteria, for a bike trail? List four criteria below, and support your answer with evidence from the three sources.

_____

_____

_____

_____

_____

_____

2 Which of the following statements represents an accurate claim that one could make based on the three sources?

    a. Mountain biking trails are only available to professional mountain bikers.

    b. Cyclists will never use trails that are near towns.

    c. Cycling is dangerous.

    d. Cyclists consider many criteria when picking a trail.

3 Which evidence below best supports your answer to Question 2?

   a. "From dirt tracks to converted railroad tracks, great trails throughout the U.S. provide a variety of terrain, scenery, amenities, challenge, and overall experience for riders of differing abilities and intentions." (Source #1)

   b. ". . . road bikes have evolved significantly, and then there's the highly popular category of mountain biking, which combines . . ." (Source #1)

   c. "Located in western Colorado's high desert, Fruita offers hundreds of miles of trails that will please just about anyone looking for a thrill." (Source #2)

   d. "Here, the terrain is made up of huge rocks, making the environs look like the surface of the moon." (Source #3)

▶ Part 2 (70 minutes)

You now have 70 minutes to review your notes and sources and to plan, draft, revise, and edit your essay. While you may use your notes and refer to the sources, your essay must represent your own original work. You may refer to your responses to Part 1 questions, but you cannot change those answers. Now read your assignment and the information about how your writing will be scored; then begin your work.

Your Assignment

The deadline for the school paper is approaching, so it's time to write your article. Having created your criteria for what makes a good bicycle trail, you need to present the criteria in the form of a newspaper article that is similar to an informative essay. As you write your article, make sure that you are including information from the three sources and that you are presenting your ideas in a logical way.

Informative Essay Scoring

Your essay will be scored using the following:

1. **Organization/purpose:** How well did you state your thesis and support your thesis with a logical progression of ideas? Did you use a variety of transitions between ideas? Was your focus narrow enough to lead to a well-formed conclusion?

2. **Evidence/elaboration:** How well did you incorporate relevant information from the sources? How well did you elaborate your ideas? Did you use precise language appropriate to your audience and purpose?

3. **Conventions:** How well did you follow the rules of grammar, punctuation, capitalization, and spelling?

Now begin work on your essay. Manage your time carefully so that you can:

- plan your essay, using your notes
- write your essay
- revise and edit your final draft

Literary Analysis

Your reading teacher has assigned your class a literary analysis about a poem and a short essay. These two literary sources are both by the same author, David Kherdian.

First you will review the two literary works. After you have reviewed these sources, you will answer some questions about them. You should first skim the sources and the questions and then go back and read them carefully.

In Part 2, you will write a literary analysis in which you compare the poem and the essay.

Time Management: Literary Analysis Task

There are two parts to most formal writing tests. Both parts of the tests are timed, so it's important to use your limited time wisely.

Part 1: Read Sources and Answer Questions

Preview the Assignment

35 minutes

You will have 35 minutes to read two literary texts about an event in the life of an author. You will also answer questions that will help you plan a literary analysis.

35 minutes! That's not much time.

How Many?

How many pages of reading?

How many multiple-choice questions?

How many prose constructed-response questions?

Preview the questions. This will help you know which information you'll need to find as you read.

How do you plan to use the 35 minutes?

Underline, circle, and take notes as you read. You probably won't have time to reread.

Estimated time to read:

Source #1: "That Day" — minutes

Source #2: "About 'That Day'" — minutes

Estimated time to answer questions? — minutes

Total — **35 minutes**

This is a lot to do in a short time.

Any concerns?

_____

_____

_____

_____

Part 2: Write the Analysis

10

How much time do you have? Pay attention to the clock!

Plan and Write a Literary Analysis

70 minutes

You will have 70 minutes to plan, write, revise, and edit your literary analysis.

Your Plan

Before you start writing, decide how you will organize your literary analysis:

Point-by-Point ☐   Subject-by-Subject ☐

How do you plan to use the 70 minutes?

Estimated time for planning the essay?		minutes
Estimated time for writing?		minutes
Estimated time for editing?		minutes
Estimated time for checking spelling, grammar, and punctuation?		minutes
Total	**70**	**minutes**

Be sure to leave enough time for this step.

Notes:

_____

_____

_____

_____

Reread your essay, making sure that the points are clear. Check that there are no spelling or punctuation mistakes.

▶ Your Task

> Your reading teacher has assigned a literary analysis to the class. You are to analyze two works by the same author–a poem and a short essay by David Kherdian. You will use what you learn from the sources to write a literary analysis in which you compare the two.

After reviewing the poem and the essay, you will answer some questions about them. Briefly skim the sources and the five questions that follow. Then, go back and read the sources carefully so you will have the information you will need to answer the questions. Take notes on the sources as you read. You may refer back to your notes at any time during Part 1 or Part 2 of the performance task.

▶ Part 1 (35 minutes)

You will now read the sources. After carefully reading the sources, use the rest of the time in Part 1 to answer the five questions about them. Though your answers to these questions will help you think about what you have read and plan your essay, they will also be scored as part of the test.

That Day

by David Kherdian

Just once
my father stopped on the way
into the house from work
and joined in the softball game
5 we were having in the street,
and attempted to play in *our*
game that *his* country had never
known.

Just once
10 and the day stands out forever
in my memory
as a father's living gesture
to his son,
that in playing even the fool
15 or clown, he would reveal
that the lines of their lives
were sewn from a tougher fabric
than the son had previously known.

NOTES

Am I on Track?

Actual Time Spent Reading

About "That Day"

by David Kherdian

In many ways my father and I were strangers to each other. At home I was his Armenian son, but in the streets I was an American stranger. I'm putting this a little bluntly. I'm exaggerating. So far as I knew, children did not play games in the Old Country. Therefore I did not believe that he understood any of the games I was involved in. And then, one day, while walking home from work, along the street where we were playing a pick-up game of softball, he stopped and either pitched the ball, or picked up the bat and tried to give the ball

10 a hit. He was *intentionally* participating, he was joining in, and by doing so he was sharing with me something that was of value in my life that I did not believe had any importance in his life. I was deeply touched by this, though why I was touched, or where I was touched, or even how I was touched, was beyond my understanding at the time. Which brings me to poetry and why I write. But that's another story, and has to do with why I wrote *all* my poems, not just the one you are looking at today.

Am I on Track?

Actual Time Spent Reading

Part 1 Questions

Answer the following questions. You may refer to your reading notes, and you should cite text evidence in your responses. Your answers to these questions will be scored. You will be able to refer to your answers as you write your literary analysis in Part 2.

1 What does the word *fabric* mean in these lines from Source #1?

" . . . that in playing even the fool
or clown, he would reveal
that the lines of their lives
were sewn from a tougher fabric
than the son had previously known." (lines 14–18)

   a. arrangement

   b. cloth

   c. device

   d. machine

2 Which word from the lines of text in Question 1 best helps you understand the meaning of *fabric*?

   a. fool

   b. lines

   c. sewn

   d. tougher

3 Which of the following sentences best states an important theme about "that day," as described in the two sources?

   a. It is better to participate than to sit on the sidelines.

   b. Strangers find common ground in sports.

   c. Sharing even small experiences can add lasting value to life.

   d. Birds of a feather flock together.

4 Select three pieces of evidence from Source #1 and Source #2 that support the answer to Question 3.

    a. "Just once / my father stopped on the way / into the house from work / and joined in the softball game " (Source #1, lines 1–4)

    b. "and attempted to play in *our* / game that *his* country had never/ known." (Source #1, lines 6–8)

    c. "Just once / and the day stands out forever / in my memory" (Source #1, lines 9–11)

    d. "that in playing even the fool / or clown . . . " (Source #1, lines 14–15)

    e. "In many ways my father and I were strangers to each other." (Source #2, lines 1–2)

    f. "At home I was his Armenian son, but in the streets I was an American stranger." (Source #2, lines 2–3)

    g. "He was *intentionally* participating, he was joining in, and by doing so he was sharing with me something that was of value in my life that I did not believe had any importance in his life." (Source #2, lines 10–12)

    h. "I was deeply touched by this, though why I was touched, or where I was touched, or even how I was touched, was beyond my understanding at the time." (Source #2, lines 13–15)

5 **Prose Constructed-Response** Based on the information found in the two sources, make an inference about the influence of his father's participation in the softball game on Kherdian's reason for writing poetry today. Cite evidence from both texts to support your inference.

_____

_____

_____

_____

_____

▶ Part 2 (70 minutes)

You now have 70 minutes to review your notes and sources and to plan, draft, revise, and edit your essay. While you may use your notes and refer to the sources, your essay must represent your own original work. You may refer to your responses to Part 1 questions, but you cannot change those answers. Now read your assignment and the information about how your writing will be scored; then begin your work.

Your Assignment

Your reading teacher has asked the class to begin writing the literary analysis. Think about the two texts by David Kherdian and what you want to say about them. As you write your analysis, compare and contrast the writer's account of "that day" in his essay with his treatment of that day in the poem. As a starting point, you may want to consider why this day was so important for Kherdian. Make sure that you include quotations from both texts and that you present your ideas in a logical order.

Literary Analysis Scoring

Your literary analysis will be scored using the following:

1. **Organization/purpose:** How well did you state your thesis/ controlling idea and support it with a logical progression of ideas? Did you use a variety of transitions between ideas? Was your controlling idea narrow enough to lead to a logical conclusion?

2. **Evidence/elaboration:** How well did you incorporate relevant information from the literary texts? How well did you elaborate your ideas? Did you use precise language appropriate to your audience and purpose?

3. **Conventions:** How well did you follow the rules of grammar, punctuation, capitalization, and spelling?

Now begin work on your essay. Manage your time carefully so that you can:

- plan your essay, using your notes

- write your essay

- revise and edit your final draft

Acknowledgments

"About 'That Day'" by David Kherdian. Text copyright © 1996-2010 by David Kherdian. Reprinted by permission of David Kherdian.

"Best American Bike Trails" by Jeff Wallach from *USA Today,* April 1, 2009. Text copyright © 2009 by Jeff Wallach. Reprinted by permission of PARS International on behalf of USA Today.

"Do Zoos Shorten Elephant Life Spans?" by Virginia Morell from *Science,* December 11, 2008. Text copyright © 2008 by Sciencemag. org. Reprinted by permission of The American Association for the Advancement of Science.

"Earth" from *The Gardener and Other Poems* by John Hall Wheelock. Text copyright © 1961 by John Hall Wheelock. Reprinted by permission of Simon & Schuster.

"The Red and Blue Coat" from *Wisdom Tales from Around the World* by Heather Forest. Text copyright © 1996 by Heather Forest. Reprinted by permission of Marian Reiner Literary Agency on behalf of August House, Inc.

"Speaking Bonobo" by Paul Raffaele from *Smithsonian.* Text copyright © 2006 by Paul Raffaele. Reprinted by permission of Paul Raffaele.

"That Day" from *I Remember Root River* by David Kherdian. Text copyright © 1978 by David Kherdian. Reprinted by permission of Overlook Press

"Top Five Places to Mountain Bike" by Beth Puliti from *About.com,* http://mountain bike.about.com. Text copyright © 2013 by Beth Puliti. Reprinted by permission of About, Inc.

"White House Conference Tackles Bullying" by Mimi Hall from *USA Today,* March 9, 2011. Text copyright © 2011 by USA Today. Reprinted by permission of PARS International on behalf of USA Today.

"The White Umbrella" by Gish Jen from *The Yale Review.* Text copyright © 1984 by Gish Jen. Reprinted by permission of the Melanie Jackson Agency on behalf of Gish Jen.